For
My Family

Contents

Monologues

Scenes & Activities

<u>Feisty Fairy.</u>

Suitability: Pre Teen

Character: Elfina

Elfina lives in the forest with other fairies, but their home is being threatened as a digger prepares to tear down the trees.

What's that noise? Is it an earthquake? The end of life as us fairies know it? Oh no the noise, the noise! It hurts my ears. Where should I hide? What about under here? Hmm don't think this pile of leaves will save me. What was that? I felt the ground shake, this is scary. The forest is my home I don't want to leave, but I don't want to die either. Timber? Did you hear that? A voice calling 'Timber' who is Timber? And whoa!!! Who is that giant with a big metal arm and chattering teeth? Now I'm really scared, the Giants are taking over, destroying our homes, stamping through our forest. Right! That's it come on Elfina you can do this. Oi you, ugly features I'm talking to you. What do you think you're doing with your growling arm? Are you trying to steal our trees? Well you can't have them we live in the trunks, you are a thief! You will never get your full set of wings with that attitude. Hey big guy I'm talking to you. I'm down here! Yes that's right I'm not going to let you scare me anymore!

Jack

Suitability: Pre Teen

Character: Annie

Annie tries to come to terms with losing her first pet.

I'm sorry I wasn't there for you when you needed me most. Momma said you went quietly and wouldn't have felt anything, that's something. I brought you your favourite, it's a bone and I've just put this pretty ribbon around it. I had this ribbon in my hair when momma sat me down "Honey" she said. "I have something very difficult to tell you." She didn't need to tell me though cos I just knew. That day when the school bus pulled up and I jumped down onto the pavement you didn't run to me, there was silence and I knew. I knew that no barking, and no friendly face to meet me from the bus meant there was something wrong. "It's ok Momma" I said. "You don't have to say it out loud, I already know" and a single tear trickled down her face. I didn't cry I just sat there being brave for Momma, but to be honest right now sat here talking to you I don't feel quite so brave. Momma said its ok to cry, that sometimes it's important and can make things better. Oh Jack I'm so sorry I wasn't there that day, please forgive me. I will never get another pet, Momma said I can have whatever I want, but I

8

won't, I won't replace you. You were my best
friend and you will live here in my heart
forever. I love you Jack.

My Friend Henry

Suitability: Pre Teen

Character: Lily (Sock puppet required)

Lily tries to reassure her sock puppet Henry that his brother who has gone missing is probably just on holiday.

My mum said "It's just a sock Lily," Just a sock? How many socks have you seen with eyes? Look at Henry's big gorgeous black eyes, so I said to Mum "How many socks do you know that can see just like you and me?" She sighed and went to make tea.

Henry is my best friend, he used to have a twin brother called Shamus but he's been missing for a few weeks now. He says I make him feel like a pair again. "I'm sure Shamus has just gone on a nice holiday" I said to Henry reassuringly, but I'm not sure I believed that myself. Shamus was the quiet one and he was very clumsy, he tried like Henry to avoid dangerous situations, like the Washing machine for instance but he wasn't as street wise as Henry and between you and me I fear the worst.

Ssh! Keep that to yourself here comes Henry now. "Hi Henry" you look smart today, (He whispers in Lily's ear) Oh wow that's great can I come to the party too? (Whisper) What do you mean it's just for people like you?

(Whispers) that is not true Henry you're just like me, you're beginning to sound like my Mum. (Whisper) You're missing Shamus? I know you are it must be tough but I can be your other half, we can be a pair. (Whisper) Why not? I know we aren't identical looking but we have the same sense of humour. What do you call an Alligator wearing a vest? An Investigator. Why aren't you laughing? Are you really so sad without Shamus? Well can't you at least try to have fun? I'm your friend too, and it's rude not to laugh at someone's jokes. Well if you're going to be like that and stay miserable just because Shamus has taken a little vacation then I think it's time you went on a trip too! (Pulling the sock from her hand) Mum! I've got some dirty washing!

<u>Peter Pan in Wonderland</u>

Suitability: Pre Teen

Character: Peter Pan

Peter finds himself unexpectedly in
Wonderland where he meets Alice.

How did I end up here? I asked to be dropped
off in Neverland. NEVERLAND! Not
WONDERLAND! This is such a strange
place. Everyone seems a little, well unhinged
if you know what I mean? They make Captain
Hook look positively sane. I was thinking I
could just fly out of here but for some reason
there seems to be no magic in this land, I'm a
little incapacitated. Where is Tink when you
need her? Wait a minute who is that pretty girl
over there? Wendy? Wendy it's me Peter.
Oops sorry I thought you were my friend
Wendy... Oh, well nice to meet you Alice. Can
you help me get out of here? Are you a pixie?
Do you have any pixie dust?... A girl! My
Wendy is a girl I haven't met many other girls
before....You need to get home too. What was
that? ...A Queen? Maybe she can help us get
home. Wait, she doesn't seem too friendly.
What is a guillotine?.... So I'm just going to
hide behind this mushroom.

Extraordinary.

Suitability: Pre Teen

Character: Ellie/Eddie

Ellie/Eddie wishes that there was something special about her/him like the others in her class.

Staring out with a blank sheet of paper in front of me. That's all I can do, for once I have nothing to say. 'Write a report on your biggest achievement' Mrs Holt said as she flicked her nose a couple of times, yes you heard me right she has this habit, she holds her fore finger pointing upwards and from right to left flicks the end of her nose. I swear to God that nose vibrates! I can hear it move from side to side as it wobbles as if it's made of rubber. It entertains the class daily and we never get bored of holding our rulers out protruding from our nose, then twanging it as hard as we can. Anyway, we have to write about ourselves, something we are proud of achieving. But what if your biggest achievement is getting up for school on time or making your own breakfast? You see there's nothing remarkable about me. Not like Suzy Norman who wins every race on sports day, her egg has never and I mean never fallen off the spoon! Or like Jenny Rae Toussant who can speak two languages and lived in

13

France for three whole years, or like my sister who is literally good at everything. My mum always says 'She has the voice of an Angel,' and she does, I love to hear her sing. I'm not like anyone else. I'm just plain old me who helps Mum around the house, takes the dog for a walk and likes to listen to the TV. Mrs Holt says if it's easier for me I can do my homework as a recording, but I've been learning Braille for the last two years and I won't take the easy way out. You don't become extraordinary by avoiding challenges. So watch out Suzy Norman I don't have to stick my egg to the spoon to be special.

<u>My World.</u>

Suitability: Pre Teen

Character: Isaac/Imogen

*Isaac/Imogen talks about his/her beloved pet
Connie and her trip to see the vet.*

If I close my eyes I can see her, it feels real.
We are running together through the fields
without a care in the world. She is my whole
world, she is the only one I can rely on. When
we are out in the countryside I feel happy and
free, and sometimes when I feel sad she is
there for me. A cuddle is all that I need for me
to feel me again. My best friend may not be
able to answer all my questions but often it's
not answers I need, what I need is a
dependable friend and that is what Connie is,
or should I say was.

It was a regular trip to the vet, an inoculation
which we went for each year. She was healthy
or so I thought. Perfect in my mind and I stood
next to my Mum holding her paw, stroking her
soft fur, keeping her calm. The vet was
friendly she smiled in a comforting way that
took my fears away. Connie seemed unfazed
by the needle that headed her way and she
didn't even flinch. She was braver than me, I
hate needles and I've always cried at the
thought of a visit to the doctors, but my best
friend was the bravest.

The vet gave Connie a full check up and asked to speak to my Mum outside of the room, I stayed with Connie and I could hear whispering. Later on that day as I was getting ready for bed my Mum asked to speak to me. She held my hand and I listened to the worst news I had ever heard, a heart defect she said, my Connie, my world was sick.

No! I don't believe you. Connie is brave and strong and she will never leave me. She's my world! My Mum held me tight. She was with me for a few months after this and we spent every second together. Then she was gone.

I open my eyes and it is quiet and I am alone. My world is different. Mum said time heals and when the new puppy arrives I'll feel better, but I won't. Connie will never be replaced. She will always be my world, even if now she only appears when I close my eyes.

I Won't Choose.

Suitability: Pre Teen

Character: Robert/Ruth

Robert/Ruth is asked to decide who he/she wants to live with after his/her parents divorce.

You want me to choose? What? You mean like pick? But I don't want to pick. I won't pick! I love them both, I love them both as much as each other. I love them both the same. I don't want anything to change, things are fine! They're fine. I never even heard them argue, so I don't really know why we are here. Why? Why don't they love each other? They can be friends can't they? When me and Matilda had a row about whether or not she had lent me the latest Wimpy Kid book, which by the way she had but I definitely gave her it back, we just didn't talk for one playtime then we just couldn't help it, we started giggling at one of Tommy Haywood's silly jokes and that was it, just like that, best friends again. So it's simple really, Mum just needs to laugh at one of Dads daft impressions and we can all go back to the way it was, and I won't have to choose and I can stay in my house with my family. Please, please don't make me choose.

<u>Alfie</u>

Suitability: Pre Teen

Character: Ben/Betsie

Ben/Betsie look forward to Christmas time and wintery weather as he/she gets to spend time with someone special.

I know we only have a short time together Alfie but I want you to know that you are amazing, and even though you are deteriorating every day you remain the same to me. I love getting up and seeing your big smile out of my bedroom window, but Mum says you will be gone soon and I should prepare myself. That makes me sad but I'm hoping you will be back next year. Christmas just isn't the same without you. I'm going to buy you a new bobble hat with a matching scarf, I think red would suit you best. Oh no Alfie you've lost an eye, I hope that wasn't painful. I bet that pesky dog next door had something to do with it, Mum always says 'She's just being playful, she's only a puppy,' like losing an eye isn't serious! And what is that yellow streak down your left side, oh my goodness that just isn't cool and it is certainly not being playful! It's sabotage!
  Sometimes I feel like we only have each other Alfie, you're the only one who listens to me and I know how much you enjoy our days in the snow. I don't want the sun to come

back, I can't bear to see you disappear for another year. Becoming a puddle is all you have to look forward to and I bet that dog next door will just love paddling in you, or worse. That animal has no respect.

You may be shrinking in front of my very eyes but my love for you is greater than ever. I am praying for a big freeze next winter so we can be together again, and I promise you this Alfie.... I will build the biggest animal proof barricade all the way around you. Playful puppy? I don't think so, more like devil dog! Happy New Year Alfie, see you again next year.

(Aside) I think I better save the global warming chat for another time.

<u>I'm Not Ready</u>

Suitability: Pre Teen

Character: Evan/Eva

Evan/Eva enjoy playing the saxophone and attends lessons with Miss Angela who has decided it's time he/she took his/her first grade, but Evan/Eva doesn't feel ready.

'Turn that music down!' That was my Mum's reaction to me practising my saxophone. On a positive note, no pun intended, she thought I was playing one of my CD's so I must be improving. I love playing my sax it is so relaxing after a long and slightly boring day at school. When I first started learning it was really hard and I couldn't even make a sound out of it, then I progressed to a squeak, and now apparently I sound like an actual CD. Although Mum has had a glass of wine so I'll take that compliment loosely. My teacher Miss Angela keeps saying 'Evan you're ready to take your first grade,' but I'm not. I don't like playing in front of strangers; she tells me there will be just one examiner in the room but even one unfamiliar face makes my heart race, my legs wobble and my saxophone squeak. I'm not sure why anyone would choose to be in that situation. I'm happy just playing my instrument to the four walls of my bedroom, and Chip my hamster who I'm sure runs around his wheel faster when I play. My Mum said she would give me a tenner if I do it, surely that's bribery, although there is this awesome computer game I've been saving for so it's worth some consideration. I just need to work on my jelly legs and shaky fingers or I'm going to be hitting all the wrong notes and I won't sound like a CD, I'll sound like a chorus of mice squeaking their way through a poor rendition of Somewhere only we know. Mum always says a nice glass of wine steadies her nerves, apparently it's called Dutch courage, so maybe there is an answer to my predicament, yes that's it, I'm going to wait until I'm eighteen to take my grade one examination.

My Grandma Never Sits Down

Suitability: Pre Teen

Character: Robert

Robert talks about his active Grandma who is always full of energy.

My Grandma never sits down. She's always doing jobs around the house but it's not even her house, it's mine. One day she came round, and let herself in. She's even got her own key. My Grandma also loves to iron, she even irons my underpants, and nobody wants to touch my underpants, people don't even look at them! I don't need my underpants straightened. She says that her job is to look after us but what kind of job is that? When I'm older, well not quite as old as Grandma, I want to be a fast sprinter who beats Bolts world record. The only record my Grandma is going to beat is how many underpants can be ironed in one minute, sounds boring and totally not cool. My Grandma has more energy than all the family put together, when she isn't doing jobs she takes me out for sports, bowling, cinema and swimming. She is also very competitive when we play squash she always beats me. She says "I always had the potential to be a professional, but you my boy can be even more." I've always been Grandma's little champ, I think I'm her favourite but don't tell my sister.

Can I tell you a secret, I've been worrying lately, what about the day when grandma gets too old and runs out of energy. I mean she says she's going to out live us all but what if that's not true? Even though my Grandma can be annoying with all the jobs she does I can't live without my active Grandma. I think she has super powers but everyone thinks otherwise, but let me tell you there is only one person who can iron 534 pair of underpants in one minute. In fact she's trying to beat the record now 532, 533, 534, 535! Yay! Grandma you've done it. You should probably sit down for a few minutes before you get too tired. 'Tired is not in my vocabulary' she replies. Yes I know you've got jobs to do but you've been doing house work for four hours. I don't know how she does it all! Yep there she goes putting more underpants in the washing machine. No wait Grandma not in there, that's the dishwasher.

Written by Evan Watkinson
Edited by Joanne Watkinson

Geronimo!

Suitability: Pre Teen/Teen

Character: Tom/Tia

Tom/Tia is preparing to do a bungee jump to impress his/her friends who have dared him/her.

You can do it, you CAN do it! Stay focused. Eyes open? No definitely eyes shut. I can't believe I've let them persuade me, when will I learn that accepting a bet does not turn out well. (Shouting below) I will jump, when I'm ready! Ok breathe. I'm ready, I am ready. I'm going to do it..... Any minute ... After 3.....2......2.....2.... (Turning to the extreme sports tutor)
So the elastic can hold a tonne you say? And it's never snapped before, right?

   I remember as a child my mother taking me up a lighthouse to see the sights, all those steps, climbing higher and higher as my heart raced faster and faster. I never did see those views she talked about, my eyes were tightly shut. A bit like now, I can't look down because if I do my heart may actually stop!

   I can feel my friends all staring up at me; they think it's all really funny. They always dare me because they know I'll attempt it. Not because I want to but because I don't want to lose face. You see I want them to like me; I want them to think I'm cool. I mean I'm not, cool that is, I'm very uncool, at least I was at my old school and when I moved here to Devon, home of extreme sports, I decided I wasn't going to be that geeky kid anymore. So you see I feel like I have something to prove. So I will jump, I think, and I won't lose face but I will keep my eyes tightly shut. Ok I'm ready. 1, 2, Geroni....No! No! It's so high up here. 1, 2, Geronimmmm...No! Don't lose face, do not lose face. 1, 2, Geroni....I think I'll just stick with being the local geek.

Evacuee

Suitability: Pre Teen/Teen

Character: John/Jane

John/Jane is an evacuee who is making the train journey to meet the people who will be taking care of him/her whilst the war continues.

I stood on the platform feeling terrified but putting on a brave smile for the benefit of my mother who wasn't as good at covering up her sadness. I could see the pain in her eyes. The journey on the train was long and quiet, everyone wrapped up in their own thoughts, their own heart break. Mother had promised it was only going to be for a short time but I wasn't sure, I hadn't been away from mother for even one day my whole life. I had gotten used to not seeing father with the war taking him away, taking all the fathers away. Mother and I had always been there for each other in my Fathers absence and I worry about how lonely and scared she will be without me to care for. I will write to her everyday and draw her pictures of the countryside, of the cows, tractors, endless fields and all the other things I will be seeing for the first time.

   The train pulled up to the platform slowly as we arrived in Yorkshire, our new temporary families lined the station platform and I disembarked wondering which family would be mine, at least for the foreseeable future. I can't help but look around for the friendliest face in the hope that they will be my new hosts. I scan the line of adults before me and their children, then I spot her, she's the most beautiful lady I have ever seen. She has a lovely welcoming smile and I quickly pray. Dear Lord, just a quick prayer to ask you to let this beautiful and friendly lady reach out for me. I think we are a perfect match and I would really appreciate it if I could go and stay at her home. Amen.

She steps forward and I hold my breath, Please call my name, please. But she doesn't and my heart sinks with disappointment.

<u>Little Bo Peep-The report of the missing
sheep.</u>

Suitability: Pre Teen/Young Teen

Character: Bo Peep

*Bo Peep has lost her sheep Barbra and Bartie,
she searches Nursery Rhyme Land and meets
several characters along the way.*

Hello Humpty, have you seen my sheep? Oh
dear it's not like them to just wander off like
this (calling) BaaaaaaBra, BaaaaaaBra! Oh
dear, Barbra doesn't like the cold and she will
be so frightened, and Bartholomew is afraid of
the dark. I must find them before the sun goes
down. I thought you might be able to see them
from your wall Humpty, please will you keep
a look out for me and if you see them let me
know egg-sactly where I can find them. Oh no
Humpty it wasn't an egg joke I promise, I
wouldn't be yolking at a time like this (She
giggles). Oh Humpty cheer up old fellow, you
have a very important job to do and you could
be the hero of the story. Thank you Humpty
now I really should be on my way, stood here
chatting to you wont find Barbra and
Bartholomew now will it. Baaaaa-bra, oh
Baaaa-bra, Bartholomew! Come out, come out
where ever you are. Oh hi Miss Muffet, have
you seen my sheep? Someone stole your curds
and whey? Oh my! Well I can assure you that
Barbra and little Bartie don't like Curd. But

maybe Humpty saw the culprit from his wall?
Goodbye. Well there is only one last thing I
can do, I will have to call the authorities. (She
takes out her phone) Is that the home of the
king's men? I request your immediate help, I
seem to have misplaced my sheep and I'm
getting rather concerned about their
whereabouts. Immediately? Well that is a
fantastic service, I appreciate it. I will call you
back in a little while. Baaa-bra, Bartie! Oh
dear, where could they be? Oh hello Mr Cow,
I don't suppose you've seen any sheep
wandering in the fields? And by the way
congratulations on your world record jump.
The Moon! I say Mr C, that is impressive. But
I'm sorry to hear about Dish, I know you two
were close but if you ask me if I'm surprised?
Well the truth is no I'm not. Dish and Spoon
were a match, it was inevitable. Anyway I
can't stop to gossip I must find my sheep
before dark. (She pulls out her phone) Hi it's
Bo I'm just wondering if you have had any
luck with finding my beloved sheep. Oh my
days! Yes I completely understand. Mr Cow,
you will never believe it, such tragic news. On
the way to look for Barbra and Bartie all the
kings horses and all the kings men found
Humpty in a state of disrepair, they think he's
taken a tumble off the wall and he is in pieces.
They are doing their best to put him back
together and egg-stract the evidence. Oh my,
no time for jokes Bo. I think I'll go home and
knit him a get well jumper, suddenly missing
sheep doesn't seem quite so important.

Winner

Suitability: Pre Teen/Teen

Character: Fiona/Freddie

Fiona/Freddie is a budding athlete preparing to race her/his rival.

I hear the voice of my coach in my head 'Fiona don't be psyched out be anyone'. Right, Fiona, stay calm you can do this. But as I look around at the other athletes I feel the butterflies start. Stay focused and keep stretching! But I feel her eyes looking at me. Then over she comes or should I say struts, 'What's your PB?' I look up and without thinking, actually my new personal best will be performed today, did you hear her tut at me and walk away, less of a strut now Abigail Asquith! I have no idea where my new found confidence has come from. Okay so it was verging on cocky but I've had years of that from her, and she has successfully psyched me out on most occasions. Well this is it, time to make my way to the line, I keep telling myself I can win but self doubt is pretty strong and it niggles at my new found confidence. I'm having an exhausting internal battle as the starter holds up his pistol. Look at Asquith glancing across at me from lane three. Maybe, just maybe she actually feels a bit threatened. As we enter the starting blocks I feel strong and powerful, I'm going to bring you down

Asquith. Fiona Steadman is the only winner of
this race.

<u>Loves me, loves me not.</u>

Suitability: Pre Teen/Teen

Character: Emily

Emily is in love with Tom and is trying to work out if the feeling is mutual.

He loves me, he loves me not, he loves me, he loves me not, he loves me, he loves me not, NOT! Dumb flower. I don't need a dumb flower to tell me what I already know. I mean the way he looks at me across the play ground, it's as if I'm the only girl in the world. He picked me for his team in games last week. Ok so he didn't pick me first but I guess he didn't want to make it too obvious. Alright, alright so he didn't pick me second or third but I was the first girl to be picked, so really that says it all. In class the other day Miss said 'Emily what is the answer to this sum?' She pointed to the white board, and my hands started to sweat, I could feel my heart racing. The numbers looked so jumbled and my brain wouldn't think, all eyes were on me, I heard giggling from behind me, but there was no answer I could muster up. Then suddenly I heard the most beautiful voice, 'The answer is one hundred and twenty seven Miss.' 'Thank you Thomas,' said Miss Dobson. I felt a sense of relief and now my heart was beating fast for another reason. I knew it Tom Barnes loves me. He came to the rescue, my hero saved me from total humiliation. A boy would only do that if he liked a girl, right?

Only two weeks until Valentine's Day, I've started work on Tom's home made card, then he will know how much I care. I'm looking forward to seeing what he gets me, a chocolate heart maybe? Or a great big teddy bear with the words 'be mine' embroidered on the front? I'm so excited, I'm going to get my first ever boyfriend. You see dumb daisies can be wrong.

The Break Up

Suitability: Pre Teen/Teen

Character: Sam

Sam is trying to deal with his/her parents break up.

'You're allowed to be angry' my mother said. I don't need her permission. I don't feel anger, I don't feel sad. I feel nothing! Just emptiness mixed with a feeling of betrayal, betrayed by the people I love the most, the two people I most rely upon. But now there wasn't two people to rely on and trust, there was no trust, not anymore. They didn't trust each other; they didn't even love each other, so how could I trust them. Now there was just me, I could only rely upon myself.

How could you do this, you've ruined my life, you've ruined our family. I don't want to live in two houses; I don't want to move anywhere. I want to stay in my bedroom, in my house, in my village. I want to go to my school, with my friends where I'm happy. Please Mum, don't do this. Can't you just try to get along? I promise to be well behaved, yes I know it's not me Mum, I know it's not my fault deep down but then why does it feel like it is? But sometimes I think it is partly because of me. Have I been too much of a handful? Too loud? Too annoying? Too much in the way? Have I? Because I can change and then Dad will come home and we can be a family again, just the three of us. Don't tell me I will understand one day, because I won't! I really won't!

You just need to remember the good times. Christmas, that was a happy time, last Christmas when you bought Dad that gold watch, he loved it remember. He always wears it, even now. And he bought you that perfume, your favourite. You still wear that don't you? Stop treating me like I don't understand, I do understand. I know what Dad did Mum, I heard you arguing. He said he was sorry didn't he? Didn't he? Forgive and forget that's what you've always told me. Please Mum just forgive him, I need you both.

There's Nothing Jolly About Me.

Suitability: Pre Teen/Teen

Character: Old King Cole

Old King Cole, is in a therapy session to address his feelings towards being a royal.

Ok let me set the record straight the name is King Cole, so can we have less of the Old! And while I'm at it you may as well know there's nothing jolly about me. Oh I'm so sorry did I burst the majestic bubble? Well let me tell you, I fulfil all my royal duties with a big fat smile on my face and a polite royal wave. I stop to talk to the people, I'm well spoken and think carefully about every sentence so it doesn't come back to haunt me, but what I'm really thinking about is... is.... how I'd like to be sat at home watching Netflix with a cup of cocoa and some fried chicken.

So here I am talking to you, knowing you can't do a thing about it. Therapy can't work on royalty can it? Because let's face it, I'm not allowed to change. There's the real me and the royal me, two personalities! It's draining pretending to be a jolly old soul. To tell you the absolute truth, because let's face it that's what I'm supposed to do when I'm talking to you, right? I'm miserable. The only people on this planet I can call friends are three fiddlers, Tom, Dom and Derek, and they work for me at the palace so they don't really count do they, they're friends because they're paid to be. I can't make real friends because I can't leave the palace without a whole lot of pre-planning and an entourage Beyonce would be proud of.

Am I lonely? Have you not been listening? I'm trapped in this world of royal visits, of minding my P's and Q's, of misery. It's a fake world. And I'm expected to find this perfect wife, a suitable Queen. Perfect? There's no such thing. Every girl I meet is only interested in jewels and living in luxury. I don't want luxury, I want normal. I need to know what it's like for my soul to feel jolly. What even is jolly? And as for old, I'm certainly not OLD! The only old thing about me is this fake old smile that I carry around with me day in, day out. But believe me there is nothing in my world to feel happy about. As I said before there's nothing jolly about me.

Gran Says.

Suitability: Pre Teen/ Young Teen

Character: Ethan

Ethan takes advice from his Gran over a girl he likes at school.

Gran says that actions speak louder than words, so why is it despite a dozen red roses and a love letter that took me three whole days to write she still hasn't said one single word to me. I've even given her a diamond ring, well a diamond looking ring, my pocket money doesn't stretch to the real thing but my Gran says it's the thought that counts. Maybe living with Gran has made me a little old fashioned but she says I'm a gentleman and my mother would've been proud of me. So how is it that my actions are not speaking to Sophie Louise Jeffries? I left the flowers by her locker, she couldn't have missed them, I'd decorated the label with her name and different coloured hearts, that's what girls like don't they? Do you think she will ever want to go out with me? Yes but you would say that your my Gran. But am I handsome in anyone else's eyes?

 I posted the love letter straight through the letterbox of her house, it's one of those outside ones with a little key to unlock and retrieve your mail. I know she received it because I hid behind the bushes of the house next door and waited. Her mum opened the mailbox and I heard her shout 'Sophie you've got mail and it's covered in pretty little unicorns'. I'd heard from Katie Sue that Sophie liked unicorns and all things mystical. So I know she got it. Gran do you think the ring was a step too far? She didn't have it on at school today, I know because I followed her to her form room. I pretended I had a message for her teacher. Gran am I coming on too strong? Did Grandad send you nice gifts? So it worked for you, he sent you letters everyday during the war and you replied to each one didn't you? You must've really loved each other, maybe you could show them to me. I could get some much needed inspiration from them.....What did you say Gran? I've got mail. It must be from Sophie, my first ever love letter. (He opens the envelope). Gran what's a stalker?

The Audition

Suitability: Pre Teen/Teen

Character: Sally

Sally attends an audition, she is nervous as she doesn't feel like she stands out like all the other girls.

I can feel my heart beating faster, sometimes I wonder why I put myself through it. I've had thirty two auditions in total and only one recall, but something tells me this will be the big one. What is she looking at? Can she tell my legs have gone to jelly? Maybe she's trying to psych me out, well that's good she must see me as a threat. No don't be ridiculous Sally! You're over thinking things again. Ok Sally Ann and breathe (She takes a series of deep breaths). This is the worst bit, the wait, the looks, the game faces. You always get the pretentious ones "This is my third audition this week, the last director I worked with said I had something special." blah, blah, I can see two things he thought were special about her! But me well I know I'm pretty....pretty plain that is. I don't stand out in any crowd, why would I stand out here with all these beautiful, experienced girls. I know I should probably give up the dream but I just can't seem to let go of what I've always wanted. Sally isn't even a stand out name. You see her there, the one with the blonde hair and perfect teeth, yes that

one, well her name is Bluebell Constantine
Viola. Yep real name apparently, and the
perfectly groomed brunette in the corner her
name is Lightning Storm. So you see 'Sally
Ann' doesn't really make me unforgettable.
It's not about pure talent these days is it? It's
about who you know, what you know and
what daft hippy name your parents gave you.
Nothing against hippies of course, I'm all for
peace, love and all that but sometimes I think
parents must've planned ahead. Planned their
new borns path to stardom, starting with a
quirky name that's totally unforgettable.
Listen to me rabbiting on, it's just my nerves,
I'm so rude I haven't even asked your
name....Tinkerbell… as in Tinkerbell and
Peter Pan? (Awkwardly) Aww what a
beautiful name. Well Tink, do you mind if I
call you that? Oh okay, Tinkerbell it is then!
It's been nice talking to you but I think I heard
someone call my name, my exceedingly
boring name. Break a leg!

Excitement is Exhausting!

Suitability: Pre Teen/Teen

Character: Amy

Amy's Mum treats her to an evening at the theatre watching a ballet. Although Amy loves to dance she isn't so keen to watch it and finds it hard to appear interested.

Do I look excited? (To member of the audience) Sir it was a rhetorical question! Do I? Of course I don't because I'm not.' It will be the most exciting day of your life so far' my mum announced. Interesting she put so far on the end of that sentence; even she didn't think it would be the most exciting day of my life ever.

You see, I loved going to my dance classes every Saturday morning, I loved wearing the pink leotard and tights and my precious ballet shoes, the feeling I got when I danced around the studio was like no other. So I guess I could understand why my mum thought a trip to the theatre to watch a ballet would be the perfect gift for my birthday. 'Thanks Mum' I said feigning excitement, but inside I was simply disappointed. You see I loved to dance but my idea of fun wasn't watching others do the same; quite frankly watching others do ballet was boring. But my Mum thought she had come up with the best present idea ever and I didn't want to upset her, so I smiled and faked enthusiasm for the idea.

And so here we are the night of my birthday treat, Mum spent hours getting ready and she refused to let me wear my jeans, so to add to my misery I had to wear a dress. We enter the theatre, it's old but Mum calls it ornate, whatever that means. We take our seats on the front row, yep the front row! More fake excitement required. Even the dancers would be able to see my bored expression. The music starts and Mum glances at me with a huge smile on her face, I smile back and try hard to keep that smile painted across my face, but I wasn't too good at that. The accompaniment is so slow and it's making my eye lids feel heavy, oh no sleepiness has kicked in and I can't fight it! Another smile at mum to reassure her and now I'm going to just rest my head on my arm, get myself comfy. Suddenly I hear Mum say 'Wow! That was just wonderful wasn't it darling?' 'Sure was!' I try to wake myself up. Would I like an ice cream, ice cream? I thought we would be going home. 'Erm no thanks Mum,' it's the what? The interval? And then it dawned on me, there was more to come, we are only half way through! Faking excitement is exhausting!

The following two monologues are inspired by the play A Striking Friendship.

Hard Times

Suitability: Pre Teen/Teen

Character: Alison Samson

Alison talks about her family in light of the 1984 miners strike.

It was just the way things were, but it was tough, tough times for everyone. My Mum didn't realise it but really she was the strength behind it all, she was the rock holding up our family. My Mum worked hard every day of her life keeping us all happy, organised, fed and watered. After all it was the eighties and it wasn't uncommon for wives to stay at home. Dad went out to work and Mum didn't. I loved coming home from school to her home cooking, she made a mean lasagne and we had that every Friday like clockwork. Life was good, well for a while anyway. Mum was a Queen fan, she adored Freddy Mercury, she said his moustache made him look sophisticated, she said he was the only man she would leave Dad for. She was yet to discover his alternative interest.

My Dad is a strong man in many ways, he worked hard and has strong values. He takes life seriously, and what he believes, he believes and no amount of debate or discussion would change his mind on any topic. But most of all political issues which us kids just find boring. There is no doubt in my mind that he was no fan of Thatcher and he expected us all follow suit. Which in the climate of the eighties living in a Yorkshire mining village it wasn't too difficult. My Dad had worked down the mines all his life, it's all he knew, and now we had nothing and I mean nothing. We literally did not have a thing.

My brother Stuart thought the world had ended when Mum took his Walkman to the pawn shop, he's going through a selfish phase, Mum calls it puberty.

Shelley my older sister spends all day everyday practising routines to her favourite Wham songs, and learning the lyrics by rewinding the cassette tape over and over again. It can get really annoying, basically her life consists of Smash Hits magazine, spiral perms and boys. I'm not quite sure where I fit in, I'm not like any of them. I just spend my days hanging out with Kevin or at least I did. He's my best mate, or should I say was until my Dad put a stop to that. Apparently his Dad's a scab and because he went back to work and crossed the picket line. We aren't allowed to see each other anymore. I'm supposed to blame one person for everything including my lack of friends, lack of food, the missing TV and the general misery in this community, and there's no surprises for guessing who that is. Thanks a lot Maggie!

Suitability: Pre Teen/Teen

Character: Alison Samson

Kevin asks Alison on a date. She is suspicious of how he can afford it and it soon comes to light that his father has crossed the picket line.

The cinema? What you want to take me on a date of something? Well I do like Han Solo, so maybe... no I can't. Look no offence Kevin but we haven't got any money. You'll pay? But your family are skint too. Maybe we can just go to the park, listen to your walkman or something. Oh no here we go, avoid eye contact it's the BMX bandits, Kev don't say a word let me handle it.

Hey you, don't call him that! Get lost, why do you always pick on him he's never done anything to you. Go on do one! Go and push around someone your own size. Are you ok Kev? Don't turn on me, I wasn't trying to save you! I did save you. They'd have kicked your head in Kevin if it wasn't for me they're thugs. What did they mean when they called you Scabatha? It can't have been nothing, they seemed pretty angry with you. You can tell me anything Kev we are supposed to be best mates. Your Dad has what? But he can't, that's crossing a picket line Kevin, don't you realise what that means? So that's why you could afford to take me to the cinema. Well I won't go, I don't care if they're showing the entire Star Wars trilogy back to back, my parents will lose the plot when they find out. I won't use money from a scab! And neither should you. I'm sorry that your Mum is ill and I get that your Dad thinks the money will help her, but this is about more than just your family. Don't you get that? Kevin I'm sorry but I can't see you anymore. It's not just going to be the issues between our parents, it will be the whole community. You can kiss goodbye to life as you know it. I'm sorry, see ya Kev.

Cyber Torture

Suitability: Teen

Character: Jemma

Jemma is struggling to deal with bullies at school.

There's nothing wrong Mum, why don't you believe me? I am happy; yes school was fine, everything is just fine. I don't need to talk and I don't need a cup of tea! Back off I've got homework to do. I don't lock myself away why would you say that? I just like hanging out in my room that's all. I need space Mum, I'm not a little girl anymore, chocolate can't fix things. That's not what I meant, nothing needs fixing, it was hypothetical! Please just leave me alone.

How dare you, how dare you stand there and call me names, oh wait you don't say those vile words to my face do you? Because you are a coward, you hide behind your laptop spending endless hours entertaining yourself with creating new ways to hurt me, and encouraging other weak minded people to join you! You have nothing else to fill your time with because no one really cares about you, that's the truth! You hurt me to mask your pain. Well I feel sorry for you, but it stops now! So take yourself off to your gang of nasty little creatures and get yourselves a life! A real life, in real time! That's what I want to say to her, but I don't, I can't. I feel incapacitated when I'm around her and her flock of pathetic little sheep. I'm angry inside but I can't let it out. I just seem to take my anger out on my family; I haven't found a way to confide in anybody about what is happening to me, I feel too humiliated. I don't know how much more I can take, the torture is relentless, I am ignored at school and tormented at home. I know I shouldn't look at the comments but I can't seem to help it. The only way would be to not have a phone or laptop, but I can't, my Mum would wonder why I'm not answering to her calls and I really don't want to worry her by telling her of my pain. There is this teacher at school who is kind and although I think she probably pity's me, she's the only one I could possibly talk to, I'm just scared it makes things worse. I've had a ruck sack packed for several weeks now, it's hidden under my bed, I keep it there next to a rope, because I know there are only two real options for me, run away or to leave this world for good.

<u>Dear Jenny</u>

Suitability: Teen

Character: Ellie

Ellie returns from school one day to face her distraught mother sobbing over her husband's infidelity.

I was walking home from school just chatting and laughing with my mates when a strange feeling came over me. Nothing's wrong I kept saying to my best mate Suzy, but a chill went down my spine. I picked up the pace, I need to get home Suzanne, she looked at me confused and I began to run.

   I found my mum sobbing in the kitchen on the floor. I thought we had been burgled; every single piece of crockery was smashed. Then I saw the letter on the side, it was addressed to my Mum, from my Dad.

Dear Jenny,
I'm sorry it's come to this. I've tried to hide my feelings but I can't live a lie any longer.

I didn't need to read anymore, I knew, I'd been expecting it. It happened last New Year's Eve, we always went around to my Aunty Shell's house for a family party. The adults always got a bit tipsy and Dad would always let me have a small glass of bubbly at midnight, I didn't really like it but it made me feel grown up. We stayed later than usual this year as Mum had had one too many and had fallen asleep on the sofa. All us kids were playing on my cousins X-box, I decided to go outside and get some air and as I opened the back door I saw them …..Kissing, it was Dad and Auntie Shell. My heart sank. They didn't see me and I just pushed it to the back of my mind, pretending it hadn't happened.

Tell Ellie I'm sorry the letter said. 'Don't cry Mum.' She held me tight and I held her tight right back. She was so sad and in that moment I hated him, and Aunty Shell. My own Mother's Sister. I will never understand adults, they spend their time telling children how to behave but they don't know how to treat each other. It's complicated they tell me, you know being an adult. Well it seems perfectly simple to me, be nice, that's it really, love your family and don't destroy them with your selfish actions. My Mum needed me more than my Dad so if we're taking sides I know which one I'm on. 'Sorry Ellie' just isn't quite enough.

<u>Dear Diary</u>

Suitability: Teen

Character: Gail

Gail confides in her diary about the troubles she's having at school.

Why do they look at me that way? Don't they know how much it hurts? How lonely I am? How much I wish I had just one person I could talk to?

   I walked to school alone as usual today and that was ok until those nasty girls began walking faster behind me, step by step catching me up. My heart started to beat faster and faster, I could hear what they were saying about me. They were talking just loud enough for me to hear, they wanted me to feel the pain of their words, all those nasty names they were calling me stabbing me straight through the heart. I picked up the pace and hoped the road ahead would be quiet so that I didn't have to stop and wait for the traffic. Fortunately it was clear, I could hear their footsteps right behind me as they caught me up but I didn't turn around, I didn't want to provoke them. A single tear ran down my face proving that I was weak just like they said I was, I was pathetic and once again I was alone.

   I reached the safety of my classroom, where I was surrounded by twenty nine other twelve year olds, none of whom had ever said one

kind word to me. I occasionally got a
sympathetic smile from Josey Monroe, she
had dealt with similar things in primary school
but even she didn't want to be my friend. I
guess she fears being back where she was a
year ago, she fears walking each day in my
shoes. I just fear being.

Diary you are my only friend.

Inner Beauty

Suitability: Teen

Character: Lynne

Lynne likes her own company, she never drew attention to herself unlike Sally Daniels who decided one day to pick on Lynne and steal her anonymity.

Can you be beautiful yet ugly at the same time? The answer is yes, and I know this to be true.

She has the longest blonde hair and the brightest blue eyes, her skin is perfect and I spend most days staring in her direction, wishing I could be more like her.
But last Monday after school I saw an ugliness that no physical perfection can disguise. It was on the school bus, I normally walk but for some reason I decided to take a ride home instead. I was minding my own business, reading my book quietly when she sat next to me. She's never even acknowledged me before and to be fair she didn't speak to me then either, at least not at first. I was invisible to her, to most people if I'm honest, but I like it that way. I've always been comfortable with my own company, I guess it's just easier. I likes that no one knew my name, that I was anonymous. But it's fair to say I've always admired Sally Daniels, she was a social

54

butterfly who everyone seemed to like, she was kind of glamorous like the stars on TV. The boys fancied her and the girls wanted to be her. Anyway this day on the bus, her phone rang. "I'm on my way, give me a break!" That was Sally's frustrated response to who ever was on the other end of the phone. She seemed to morph into someone else at that moment, she was muttering to herself angrily. I felt uncomfortable, she must've sensed this, and she turned to me, "What are you looking at Minger?" Minger! What a vile word, it's true I'm not your magazine beautiful picture perfect kind of girl, probably a little ordinary, but to be called a minger was unfair. The bus pulled up at my stop, excuse me Sally, she laughed, I mean really laughed in my face. "You want to get past Minger?" And with that she pushed me, as I fell I heard the raucous laugh of the entire bus and suddenly in that moment I was no longer invisible. Do you know what? That experience, on that Monday afternoon made me realise invisibility is a gift, Sally wasn't beautiful she was ugly and her ugliness stole my anonymity. Life hasn't quite been the same again. Kids see me, but for all the wrong reasons. They laugh at me, call me names and taunt me over my looks. But I know that if I chose to I could put make up on to make myself pretty, Sally Daniels had an inner ugliness that no amount of cosmetics could cure.

It's Here Somewhere

Suitability: Pre Teen/Teen

Character: Abbi

Abbi tries to find a letter from school she needs to give her Mum, it is lost in the depths of her messy bedroom.

I know it's here somewhere, I can remember putting it away in a safe place. I just can't remember which safe place. What do you mean it's a mess? Mum I've told you I like to organise my room in a certain way. This pile here is my dancing stuff, this here is school stuff, over here is weekend stuff, under there is a box of memories and in this corner is a neat pile of clothes that I've worn but haven't quite had time to transfer to the laundry basket. This over here is a pile of things I might need in an emergency and finally on top of this set of drawers is a pile I've labelled miscellaneous, yes that's right it's basically everything else I own.

Mum please don't nag I'll find it, why do schools send important letters out via the child anyway? I know the teachers are old but surely they've figured out how to use email. Maybe it's in my memory box. Aww Mum look at this, my first ever painting, move over Picasso, and look at this valentine card, I know you and Dad sent it but made me feel like I was very popular at the time, which lets face it is important in nursery school. Mum look do you remember when I sewed this teddy bear and gave you it for Christmas, one eye was a cool look for bears in those days. Oh wow! Mum here is Gran's wedding ring, and you thought it was lost. You see I may not be able to locate a dumb letter from my form tutor but I bet you're glad I'm a hoarder now.

<u>I Dated an Elf.</u>

Suitability: Pre Teen/Teen

Character: Rosie

Rosie has started dating one of Santa's helpers, but it is not going to plan.

Now don't get me wrong I really do love the holiday season, I love all the decorations, the lights, the presents and the good cheer. I am even partial to a little tipple on Christmas day with all the family. I love the whole Christmas dinner thing, the Turkey, stuffing balls, parsnips, even sprouts and the often hilarious game of charades after the Queens speech. To be honest there is nothing better than a bit of snow outside, while curling up inside by the log fire. You just can't beat that cosy feeling. I adore everything traditionally Christmas, and as the song famously says, I wish it could be Christmas every day. But let me tell you, right now I have never felt more frustrated! There is no snow, my log fire has gone out, and I feel extremely unchristmassy, if that's even a word. You would think that someone who considers Santa amongst his closest friends would be on time! If Santa was this abysmal at time keeping then there would be some very unhappy children across the world, and right now I'm one unhappy and slightly annoyed girl. I don't feel much like decking the halls or jingling any bells, if anything this should be jingling alarm bells in my head! I should've known better than to start dating an elf, Christmas this, Christmas that, always preoccupied with Christmas. Don't get me wrong I love the festive season as much as the next person, probably more but when it comes to going out I expect my dates to at least show up on time, well at least I know what to get him for Christmas.... A watch!

Enjoy the moment

Suitability: Teen

Character: Harry/Helen

Harry/Helen has told an elaborate lie about his/her exam results which has led to a surprise party and a few awkward conversations with family members.

Congratulations to me. I enjoyed the moment, but that's all it was, a fleeting moment where for once in my life I felt like I'd not let anyone down. My family were falling over themselves to shake my hand, to pat me on the back and tell me how proud they were and how bright my future was going to be, and I just went along with it. Thanks Aunt Jeanie, I'm really chuffed Uncle Bob, I know who would've ever thought it. Well truth be known I was the only one who thought it, thought it, then created the facade. It was a little white lie; I just didn't want to feel like a disappointment to my Mum. I really didn't expect the whole surprise party thing. But everyone seems so happy; it would be cruel to tell the truth now. Wouldn't it? I'll just carry on with the 'I got 3 A's and 5 B's scenario', it's nice to see the family have something to celebrate. Err no Aunt Jeanie I don't think I'm the college type, I was thinking of just getting myself a little job, you know bring some money in and stand on my own two feet. I don't really think it's throwing my future away, just maybe putting college plans on hold, you know for the time being. No Mum it's not what I want, I've never wanted to be a teacher or a doctor, don't you think you're getting a little carried away they're only GCSE's. Oh dear heart beating faster, slightly sweaty palms, lie growing, I'm shrinking. Wishing this party was over, time to come clean.

If I could just have your attention for a moment, no Mum it's not going to be a speech. But I would like to start by thanking you all for coming, oh really please I don't deserve your applause; this really was a much unexpected surprise. Erm anyway I'd like to say, well I'd like to announce that, that erm. Auntie Jeanie that's a lovely dress you're wearing. Sorry I'm a little distracted. Erm due to the unexpected results I received today which interestingly seem to have vanished, I have decided that I would like to, erm.... Retake my exams, yes that's right I'm going to do them all again, you know try to get those pesky little B's up to A's.

Ok so that went well, so now to find a school who will take on a lazy, unmotivated sixteen year old with 5 U's and an F in woodwork.

Going Solo

Suitability: Teen

Character: Craig

Craig is a musician, who despite his manager's efforts wants to remain a solo artist.

Collaboration? Erm I don't think that's such a top idea, you see I'm a solo artist. I realise I've not sold a huge amount of cd's but hey everyone starts somewhere, right? Wait, what? A boy band? Are you serious? So basically you want to manufacture me!? Well that's not happening. I've signed a contract and I'm afraid you're stuck with me and my artistry for two years. What? Where does it say that? Erm well no I didn't read the small print, yes I know I probably should've done but well I thought it was just about making music, good music, my music! Not very good, what do you mean? I had a sell out concert. Well you're wrong, I'll have you know that Malfield Village Hall is a big venue! So I've not made you any money yet but it takes time to you know build a fan base. I've had fan mail you know! Listen to this…. Dear Craig, I loved your concert, you can't go wrong with a synthesiser to cover all instruments, thanks for bringing the eighties back, Sincerely Reg. The girls love me and the boys want to be me! What do you mean 'Really?' Well maybe not all of them yet but they will, once I get out on tour. No not with my band mates, I don't have any band mates as I said before I AM A SOLO ARTIST! Look all I need is one strong Christmas hit and let's face it we'll be made for life and I'll be played repetitively every November, December and January on every music channel, on every continent! Give me some artistic licence please! I'd rather produce a cheesy festive number than a cheesy four piece boy band ballad! What's this? Are you kidding me? You want me to dress like that? No way, I can't pull off sequins and no I don't want to dress the same as three other people, I'm a S-O-L-O-I-S-T, a soloist! I work alone, just me, with no one around me, with no sequins in sight, just me a one man band!

Haunting

Suitability: Teen/Young Adult

Character: Hannah

Hannah is a ghost who thinks she is watching her own funeral.

Only the good die young, isn't that what they say? Well every cloud I suppose. It's strange standing here, or should I say floating here, which might I add is not all its cracked up to be. Yep floating here watching you all attend my funeral. I have to say I'm surprised, I mean a few of you I fully intended to come back and haunt, but maybe not quite so soon? Look at all those sad faces. Wait, is that Jerry Brunsworth, it is! My God, (looking up to the heavens) no offence, but what in heavens name is he doing here? I haven't seen him for five whole years; he's not even a Facebook friend! God Jerry, sorry, but really Jerry put that hanky away you faker! Most of you I expected to see, but I'm not quite sure why cousin Michael hasn't made it, probably one of those posh fashion shoots he does in Milan! You would think he would clear his diary for this; you only die once, at least as far as I know. Well Michael darling you are the first on my to haunt to do list! Hang on a minute, who asked Rosie McGib to read a tribute to me, just because we went to nursery together

64

and big school and got drunk a couple of times at college doesn't make us best friends. Speaking of best friends where is Jules? She wouldn't miss this, let me see, she would surely be on the front row with my family, nope not there, she wouldn't, would she? How could she? She's not here! Right now I'm offended, straight to the top of my to haunt list!

Hello, who's that? Jules? Is that you? I can hear you. Wait a minute, you can see me? Why aren't you sat down there balling your eyes out? Oh I see, this is your funeral. But I thought you'd survived the accident. I saw you on the operating table, you came around, I saw you. You followed the light, oh that's erm great I think, well for me it is, you know someone to haunt with. But really Jules I've got to ask... Rosie McGib?

No Stars on this Jacket.

Suitability: Teen/Young Adult

Character: Jenny

Jenny is a tour guide and holiday rep, she feels rather frustrated that she has not yet been awarded any stars for good work. This is largely because she isn't very good at her job.

I'd like to welcome you all to Sunfair holidays, I am your holiday rep and tour guide Jennifer, but you can call me Jenny. So here we start our journey from the airport to your luxury four star hotel, yes four stars! Beautiful beaches and as much food and drink as you can consume. Now if you look out of the window to the right you will see some lovely architecture those buildings are some of the oldest in the country. There are some wonderful stories about those constructions I can tell you. What was that sir? Oh nice to meet you Mr Thompson. Erm, let me answer that question, can I tell you about the history? Erm let me consult my notes, erm well Mr Thompson it's not actually in my script.....Oh look at that we've gone past. Moving on....Look at those stunning views, I bet you can't wait to get those flip flops and Speedo's on eh Mr Thompson? Anyway I digress. Over to your right is....What is that? (Fumbling through her notes) well apparently it dates back to the ancient Greeks. Mr Thompson another question? Hmm is it an amphitheatre? Let me see (fumbling through notes) still looking, can't find anything here. Ah look at that we've turned a corner so everyone just sit back, relax and enjoy my very prescriptive notes, which appear to have gotten a little mixed up. No straying from this script, not if I'm to achieve my stars! That's nice Mr Thompson but if you could save your questions until the end, I have a very long speech to get through and only a short journey to complete it, and if I don't I won't get my employee star, see? No stars on this jacket, oh no! Two years I've worked for this company, I've never had a day sick; I've dealt with the rude, the loud and the ignorant, but no stars for me!! Is it my fault that holiday makers don't want to know about buildings and the history of the island? Yes I know you do Mr Thompson! Is it my fault they just want to get to their destination without interruption? Interruption! Oh the irony, once again I'm side tracked! I finished the speech once, April 11th 2014, that was a moment I can tell you, proud of myself I was. Anyway to the left is... Oh look at that, it's your hotel. Here we are! Happy Holidays!

What Am I Doing Here?

Suitability: Teen/Young Adult

Character: Sarah

Sarah is trying to make sense of her untimely death.

What am I doing here? What is this place? Who was that? Where are you? I can hear but not see you, tell me where I am. No! That's not true, I'm going to meet my friend this afternoon and we are going to have a coffee and catch up. I set off this morning, I went to catch the bus at Grove Square, heading into town... That's...that's….that's the last thing I remember. Why did you bring me here? No! That's not true if I was dead I'd be like....like a .....well like a spirit .....wouldn't I? Sit where? You want me to sit and wait? What exactly may I ask am I waiting for? Because right now what I should be waiting for is the 92 bus from Grove Square to town to meet my friend who I haven't seen for two years! No I will not calm down, or be seated in your waiting room! Now tell me right now where I am and what I'm doing here, and more importantly how I can get out! ...... Ok I'm listening....I am calm! ...... I am calm.

It can't be true, please tell me it's not true, tell me anything else... You've kidnapped me, you're holding me hostage, you've demanded a million pound ransom for my release... Anything.... Anything else.... I'm not ready to die, I'm too young. Is this heaven? It's a bit dark for heaven... Oh my days! It's Hell isn't it? It is isn't it? I only took a pair of earrings, I was going to return them honest I was, but well I couldn't could I? Once I'd taken them the deed was done. Will you stop telling me to calm down! ...Oh so this isn't Heaven or Hell? Going back, yes, yes that would be great. Just rewind time or teleport me back or do whatever you omnipotent beings do. Ok I'm ready let's go. What? You're sending me back as a what?

The Beauty Treatment

Suitability: Teen/Young Adult

Character: Laura

Laura has treated herself to a facial at the local beauticians, she doesn't get the relaxing experience she hoped for.

So she says "My boyfriend just doesn't get it, I mean we've been dating for eighteen months now, eighteen months! Some people have been engaged, married, pregnant and divorced in that time. I'm not asking for much, I mean it doesn't have to be a big diamond, or even real, as long as it looks real and I can tell people it is, that's fine, people can be very judgy these days you know."

I'd gone in for a facial, that's all a relaxing facial to ease away life's stresses, I've recently had a few personal issues to deal with and I'd not slept properly for a week. It was starting to take it's toll on me so I thought I would treat myself to some 'me time' fifty five quid it cost me and they certainly didn't tell me that some nineteen year olds life story was part of the package. I'm laid on this massage bed with the sound of the sea playing from the tiny little CD player in the corner, candles burning, aromatic smells, very calm for the first five minutes. Then it started forty five minutes of

it, she barely took a breath. I didn't respond once, you'd think that was hint enough.
"His name is Ralph, not a common name is it. Probably because he's not, common I mean. He's actually very sophisticated, a bit like me. He's got his City and Guilds you know, so brains and braun as they say. I'm sure we will make perfectly beautiful and intelligent babies, you know good breeding and all that. He says I need to be patient, but why? When you've found the one, you've found the one and you know I'm obviously the one for him. Like two peas in a pod we are, does that sound soppy Lauren?" My name's Laura. "Oh sorry Laura, my best mate's called Laura. Well she was my best mate, she's not now. It's a long story…" Oh no not another long story, twenty more minutes…blah, blah, blah. I actually felt a sense of relief when it was over. "How was that for you?" She said, it took all my power to remain polite, well almost. "It was lovely thanks, but by the way judgy isn't a real word!"

<u>And the winner is….</u>

Suitability: Late Teen/Young Adult

Character: Victoria

Victoria thinks she has won the lottery and is planning her ideal wedding.

The lottery results can be heard in the background.

Yes! Yes! No way, Andy we've won a tenner! Oh my God! Wait 12, 24, 38. (Pause as she tries to catch her breath). Andy, Andy get here!

This cannot be real! Where's the remote, oh my God, I need to check again. Rewind, rewind, stop and play. 1, 4, 11, 12, 24, 38. Breathe woman, pull yourself together. Andy!!! I've imagined this moment a million times, million oh my God million, I'm a millionaire! Andy!! I've imagined this moment, haven't we all but I never really expected to experience it, and I can tell you it feels good, strange but good. No more debts, no more arguments over money. We can finally afford the wedding. Andy!! Come down here I'm going to marry you! Not like last time in that dull little registry office. We can renew our vows properly, it will be the wedding I always dreamed of. I'm going to turn up in a horse and cart, no wait a crystal encrusted carriage. It will be like Cinderella going to the ball. That's exactly what it's like I'm Cinderella and my fairy godmother is sending me to the ball. It's going to be the best party you've ever seen, Andy! Where the hell is he? Andy get down here I have the best news, you won't believe it. I will have the most beautiful gown, like those you see in the magazines. All covered in diamantes, no wait I can afford real diamonds, oh my days I can afford real diamonds! Andy get down here! We can afford real diamonds! I will sparkle from head to toe, I'll even dazzle the guests and don't get me started on the tiara, I mean crown. Andy!! Oh there you are, about time. Didn't you hear me shouting? Where've you been hiding? Sit down, you'll need to sit down. What's the matter? Why are you looking so sheepish, come here I'm about to make your day! What do I need to sit down for? It's you that needs to sit down. Okay, okay I'll sit down. (Pause)You did what!?!? Fake? The ticket's a fake? Why? What? I mean WHAT? (Pause) Funny! You thought that was a good joke, I'll give you joke! This situation begs one question, how will I pay for the divorce!

<u>The Loft</u>

Suitability: Teen/Young Adult

Character: Jez

*Jez believes the zombie apocalypse has
dawned and plans to take refuge in the loft.*

I'm telling you it was on the news, we need to
get the family together and take refuge in the
loft. Yes the loft, we need to be high up don't
we? Because of the manifestations. What do
you mean what manifestations? The zombie
manifestations Eddie, there's an epidemic,
please keep up. Yes zombies, it's on the news.
So there's no time to waste, get as many cans
of food as possible, then you need to get Mum
and Sarah and convince them to make their
way to the loft. I'm going up there now to
make it zombie proof. Eddie it's no laughing
matter, have you seen the Walking Dead? Yes
I know its fiction Eddie I'm not stupid, but
that isn't to say it can't happen. The news said
it's started down South and it's heading up
North towards us. You won't be accusing me
of having a vivid imagination when one of
those monsters have their choppers round your
neck. Quickly Eddie we are losing time.

(He gets his ruck sack climbs into the loft and
unpacks his essentials, he takes out several
tins of food but realises he can't open them

74

and he waits, starts to get agitated and plays cards)

Where on Earth is he? Wait did you hear that? It was like a moaning noise. Oh my days they've been eaten it's too late and now there's just me! No friends or family and no weapons unless you count this Nerf gun. This is worse than I thought. I'm going to have to make a run for it, but what if I'm trapped?

(He picks up the Nerf gun and heads towards the hatch, he opens it slowly)

You have to be kidding me, stop laughing, what's the big joke? What's fake news? Why would I know what date it is? Oh I see very funny, but it's past twelve noon so guess what suckers you're the April fools the jokes on you. And by the way if there ever is a zombie apocalypse there's one thing that's essential... a tin opener!

The Urge

Suitability: Late Teen/Young Adult

Character: Jason

Jason is meeting with his psychologist, he is talking about the urges he has to kill.

It's an urge, an uncontrollable urge, something deep inside. I just want to know what it feels like. I was thinking smothering with a pillow would be interesting but it would involve a lot of physical effort on my part. So maybe a bag on the head would be more stimulating to watch, you know to just sit back and watch it happen, slowly. I'm not sure what's made me this way, it's always been a fascination of mine, even when I was at school I would day dream about it. Other kids had hobbies like football and music, they would hang out and find mundane things to laugh about. I didn't understand them or their humour, it was futile. I didn't need friends anyway. My past time was reading, I read factual books about infamous people and how they made their mark. It's not infamy that drives me, I'm just curious. They say curiosity killed the cat well there's a certain irony about that as that's how it all started for me. You see I've tried suffocation before on my neighbour's cat, but I got bored so just reached for the kitchen knife, not very creative I know but it did the job. I read in one of my criminal biographies that apparently that is how many psychopaths start, but you see I'm not a psychopath Doctor Bailey. I'm not sure why I'm even here. I haven't followed through with my fantasies, well not since the cat episode. Wanting to know what something feels like does not mean it will happen. You really think I'm a danger to society? Are you scared of me Doctor Bailey? Why not? What if I decided you will be my first victim, human victim I should say. Do you think you could stop me? Will your PHD save you? Maybe you can intellectualise your way out of this situation. I'd watch your back Doctor Bailey if I was you, I don't like interfering people who think they can save me. You need to save yourself first. Where do you think you're going Doctor Bailey? I think you better sit down!

New Home

Suitability: Teen/Young Adult

Character: Neil/Nell

Neil/Nell are desperate to be rehoused by the council, he/she is discussing their supernatural reasons for wanting to move but the housing officer is reluctant to believe him/her.

Are you calling me a liar? It picked me up and levitated me above the bed. I'm telling you this place is haunted, so I need to get out. She was killed here you know, the previous owner killed his wife then took his own life. Only cowards do that I reckon, anyway so there's been some crazy going's on in the last week and now they're scaring the life out of me. What do you mean I don't look scared, I can't see them right now can I? You should've seen me last night, pale as a ghost I was. You couldn't tell the difference between the two of us! That was a little joke, you know to lighten the mood, no? Okay look they want me to move out and I'm telling you right now that I completely agree with these crazy ass spectres! So you need to rehouse me, why would I make this up? Look right here on my camera roll, did you see that light? Look again. It's not dust! It was a powerful force that lifted all nine stone of me clean off of the floor. Look again, how could I video a birds

78

eye view of my bedroom if this hadn't happened? A ladder? Now you're joking. Anyway as if I'd go to that much trouble, If I wanted to make a fake video I'd have used a special effects app, but I literally only had time to press record as the shadow appeared. Yes shadow, it started with a light, then I saw a shadow, then it raised me above the bed! I had no control over my body, I literally flew like Peter flipping Pan. This has nothing to do with a vivid imagination it has everything to do with you not wanting to re house me. It's easier for you to ignore me.

Wait! Did you hear that? I told you didn't I, there you have it proof, you've heard it for yourself. The radiator? No it wasn't water pipes, it was clearly footsteps. Trust me to get the logical thinking housing officer. Ok so I challenge you to stay here by yourself tonight. Ah the old 'I can't stay over because it's inappropriate and unprofessional' excuse. I think you may be a little scared. No I don't want to contact Reverend Hardy, it's not an exorcism I need it's one of those nice new semi detached houses on park way! I'm not getting anywhere with you am I? Fine! You can let yourself out.

Oxbridge Material.

Suitability: Teen/Young Adult

Character: Miranda/Michael

Miranda/Michael is unhappy that she/he is not making the grades at the prestigious school her father pays for her/him to attend.

What do you mean I'm not Oxbridge material? My father has spent hundreds of thousands of pounds on my education. Do they not take into account breeding anymore? Get me a super tutor, make that several, one for every subject. My parents did not choose the most prestigious British school to send me to only to be told I will not make the grade. I need to attend Oxford or Cambridge, I've told my friends. Do you know what that will do to my reputation? To my family's reputation? No of course you don't! Why would you? You're not in this circle are you? I don't suppose you have any circles. I'm not being rude it's the way it is. Are they not paying you enough here? Do they not pay salaries way above that of a state school teacher? Well I expect the value for money, do you realise what my father pays per term? It's more than you earn in a lifetime. He has high expectations and I expect a high IQ to match. Do something! Or I will have to get him to pull my funding!! I am calm! Do you realise we have friends in high places. I will not fit in at these average universities, do you realise the percentage of working class people that now attend these establishments, the worlds gone mad. Snobbery? I really don't think you're in a position to judge me, my fathers very generous donations keep you in a job. Money talks and I expect you to give me what he pays for. So I will be expecting a glowing reference and if you need to tweak my grades, then tweak them. I won't tell you again, I must be Oxbridge material, and you will make sure of that. Won't you?

<u>Evil Personified</u>

Suitability: Late Teen/Young Adult

Character: Nicky

*Nicky talks of the responsibility he/she feels
after letting his/her sister play out the day she
was murdered.*

It took all my strength to get here today, to sit
in this court room and face the man I despise,
the only way I can describe him is evil
personified. What he did to my sister is
inexcusable, despicable. It makes me
re-evaluate the country's decision to abolish
capital punishment I mean my sister can no
longer walk this earth so why should he! My
little sister was... Using the past tense is so
hard... My sister was so beautiful inside and
out, so innocent. He robbed her of that
innocence, he robbed her of a future. She
always had a smile on her face, the happiest
little girl. If only that day I had not let her play
outside on her bike, Mum had left me in
charge and I let everyone down. I let Esme
nag me 'Please' she said, 'All my friends are
allowed out. I won't tell Mum if you don't,' so
I let her and that decision will haunt me
forever. I remember so vividly her little pink
bike in the ditch looking alone and a symbol
of what was to haunt me forever. So here I sit
next to my Mother who hasn't been herself

since that fateful day. I sit here feeling a sense of guilt and anger burning through my veins as I stare at the man who stole my sister's life. He shows no remorse. How can you sit there and feel nothing! You monster! We await the verdict but I know that no punishment will be strong enough, no amount of justice will bring Esme back, and no matter the outcome my family will remain in pieces, broken. I lost my Mum that day too and I want her back, I want us all back the way we were before the devil entered our lives.

<u>Sometimes.</u>

Suitability: Young Adult

Character: Margaret

Margaret has made a tape for her husband as she is aware she has early signs of dementia.

Sometimes. That's what they said. Sometimes. That is what I have left to pin my future on. Sometimes. Sometimes I will know your name, sometimes I will remember the fun times we had, sometimes I will know you are my husband, my son, my friend. Sometimes. But not always, never always. Always isn't even part of my vocabulary, I won't even always know what always means. If this sounds confusing it's nothing compared to what is ahead, there is one guarantee and that is that for me always will be never. I can only rely on sometimes, and then as the years pass sometimes will become infrequent and I will be left to rely on occasionally. Occasionally you will walk in the room and I will know your name, but I may not know why or how I know you. I don't want you to have to go through this; you will be left with frustration, at first occasionally, but eventually always. If you are watching this tape you have got to this point and I am already lost. I want you to know that you mustn't feel the need to take care of me, I am not the girl you married, I am a woman lost not sometimes, or occasionally but always. Live what is left of your life with the memories that you are lucky enough to retain in your mind, hold them close to your heart and know that I love you always.

<u>Stood here looking at you.</u>

Suitability: Young Adult

Character: David

David is addressing Julie who he has had an affair with, he is re-evaluating his relationship and the affects on his son.

So here I am stood here looking at you and wondering if we're doing the right thing. It's not that I don't want to, I do but it's caused enough tension already. I can't just ignore all the things that have gone before, all the hurt it's caused, we've caused. Don't look at me like that, it's not that I'm breaking up with you; I just think we need to slow down. My divorce hasn't even come through yet and my son hasn't come to terms with everything, he's not ready for a new mother figure in his life. He said to me yesterday 'Dad I think you and Mum will make up and we will be a family again, stop being mean and come home.' Yes I know he doesn't fully understand but kids see what's happening, he can see how sad his Mum is and he knows that's because of me. That's unfair Julie, I care about you too you know I do, but he's my son and it's only been a few months. Ok so it's been a few years for us, but to everyone else I've only known you a couple of months. Look we could talk about this all day but the fact is the timing is

86

all wrong and I need some space to find me again, I know it sounds selfish but I've put everyone through enough and my head is spinning, two years of lies and sneaking about is exhausting. So I'm stood here looking at you wondering if I could have the ring back.

The Robbery

Suitability: Young Adult

Character: Andrew

Andrew is mourning the loss of his wife after she is shot during an armed robbery.

Just do what he says, get up slowly and don't make any noise. I'm right here honey just nice and slow.

(He kneels with hands above his head).

Try to maintain eye contact. I know you're scared but it's going to be fine just do what he says.
   Just give him the ring honey, it doesn't matter what it means to you he doesn't care, just give it to him. My heart was thumping hard in my chest and as brave as I was trying to be the truth is I was truly terrified, more for my beautiful wife than myself. I wanted to be the big man, the protector who would save the day but I was too scared to move. Give it to him, just give him the ring, but she didn't and I find myself here knelt once again but this time by her graveside. It was just a ring, it was nothing in comparison to a life. But she saw it as part of her, to hand it to him would've been a betrayal of our love in her mind, she was stronger minded than I ever was. The evil that broke

into our house that day and shot my wife in our own home fled, he fled without being caught, he fled and left behind devastation. He fled empty handed, leaving me empty inside. It seemed to take forever for the ambulance to arrive time seemed to slow, in truth it was a matter of minutes. There was nothing they could do to save her, she left me that day alone and in a world that suddenly felt surreal. So many emotions consumed me in the days to follow. Why couldn't she have just given him the ring? Anger filled every vein, but it soon turned to guilt, why wasn't it me? Why didn't he take my life? Why couldn't I protect her? Why didn't you just give him the ring? Do you know the funny thing is, it's not even real diamonds! Sure I pretended it was real, I didn't want to disappoint you, but I think you knew. I miss you, and I'm sorry I couldn't protect you.

Rest in Purgatory

Suitability: Late Teen/Young Adult

Character: Lisa

Lisa read an article in the paper which makes her thinks back to the day she escaped a dangerous man.

I can hardly believe what I'm reading, my mind flashes back to 1979 a young girl on a hot summers day playing out with all the other local kids on the street without a care in the world. We would play all day only going home to be fed and watered. That's how it was in the seventies, and it was a great way to grow up, to feel free to live fearlessly. Anyway, this one summer some builders had moved into our street to expand it with further housing. For us lot it meant exciting new places to play, foundations made great mazes, there were numerous hiding places and a big mound of earth that was great to slide down. The builders and our parents didn't seem to be bothered by our new playground. It felt good to be having a new adventure. Graham one of the builders, looking back I suspect he was the boss, asked us one day if we would like to take turns going for a ride in his digger. He didn't need to ask twice, we were all yelling ' Me first, me first.' I didn't go first, or second, in the end I didn't get a turn at all. Mum called

me in 'We are going to visit your Grandma'
she said, 'Get cleaned up.' And that's what I
did. The next day my friends were pretty quiet
about the digger rides, I thought it strange they
weren't more excited. I figured they didn't
want to make me feel jealous and nothing
more was ever said. For some reason everyone
was bored of the building site and didn't want
to play there anymore. Luckily the farm had a
new set of bails and that was always a
favourite playground when you were a
country kids. To me that summer was pretty
ordinary but looking at this paper I'm guessing
it changed some of my friend's lives forever. I
feel angry and relieved as well as guilty that it
wasn't me. I'm glad one of my friends from
summer 1979 has found her voice and that
Graham has been exposed, it's a shame his
death four years ago means he will never feel
the hand of justice. RIP Graham Rest In
Purgatory.

<u>Desperate</u>.

Suitability: Young Adult

Character: Alan/Alice

Alan/Alice is desperate for money to help with the hospital fees for his/her daughter, he/she holds up a young woman and attempt to rob her.

If you just sit still no one will hurt you. Shut up, just shut up! I said shut your mouth. No one will hear you, there's no one here. Now tell me where the safe is. I'm not mucking around here, I'll use this, I'll pull the trigger and no one will find you. No one cares, if they did they'd have helped you by now. Don't get clever, I know what I said. Even if they did know you were here they wouldn't help you. You're just a rich Toff, no one likes people like you, no real person anyway. You live in your plastic world without a care for anyone, you don't give a second thought for people like me. You think I like having to do this? You think I've done this before? Well you're wrong I've never done this before, I've never needed to. Do you hear that Toff? Need to, I need to do this its not that I want to. You see I may seem a little over emotional here and you may wonder why, but more than likely you don't care. You just want to get out of here without a bullet in your brain. I don't blame you, if I was sat in your situation I'd be the

92

same, no wait I wouldn't because I have feelings! I'd want to help people like me, yes that's right I'd want to help me. Now stop wasting my time and tell me where the safe is! This is a matter of life and death, and not just for you. Oh now you speak! Why? You want to know why? I'll tell you Toff, I'll tell you exactly why. You see this, that's a picture of my daughter, beautiful right? Well I need to see that smile again, I need money so you're going to help me. For Gods sake the safe, where the hell is it? Look at me, LOOK AT ME! Stop crying, Jeez it's not like you're skint. What do you need all that money for? Botox? The latest gadgets? Therapy? Right that's it, you've had enough opportunity, sod you, sod you (emotional) I just wanted to save her, I just wanted to see her smile. It's not even loaded, sod you.

Activities and Scenes.

Activity ideas when working with script extracts.

- Create a scene leading up to the extract.
- Create a scene after the extract.
- Write and perform a monologue for each character.
- Add step outs within the scene to give the audience insight into the characters thoughts.
- Perform the scene in different styles. E.g. As a Musical, western, Melodrama.
- Exaggerate the scene, then perform the scene at different levels of exaggeration from 1-10.
- Perform the scene at a fast pace. Then at levels of pace from 1-10.
- Perform the scene using only physicality, then add a narrator.

Activities, Scenes and Script Starters.

<u>Drama Skills to consider.</u>

- Make sure the audience can see you (Don't perform with your back to them)
- Speak clearly and project so every word can be heard.
- Don't perform your entire piece up stage (At the back) move down stage (The front).
- Try to show your character physically, you are not playing yourself.
- Be controlled during any action (Don't run around the stage).
- Keep your focus, don't corpse (Don't giggle / come out of character)
- Perform with energy this will make your audience enjoy it more.

Audience- Support everyone, clap at the end like it's the best thing you've ever seen!

Script Starters

Starting Lines for Improvisation

- It looks incredible but what is it?
- I asked you to keep it a secret
- Are you telling me that the whole thing has been cancelled?
- If you could just sit still for 2 minutes I'll explain
- Please forgive me
- I am so excited! I can't believe you did all that for me
- And I said to him "You can't tell anyone" So what does he do?!
- I'm scared, I think we should go home

Short Dialogue Extracts for use when Devising.

Students are encouraged to learn the dialogue then extend the scene.

Buried

-I've told you this is the spot.
-Are you sure?
-How many times!!!! Right here.
-Pass me the spade.
-Are you sure we should be doing this?

-Look we have been having these
conversations all week, just dig!
-How can you even be so sure?
-Dig!! Just dig!!

Are You Listening

-Are you listening to me?
-Sure.
-You're not.
-I'm not?
-No you're not.
-I'm not.
-Is there something on your mind? I mean
you're the one that invited me here.
-I know I did.
-You did.
-I did.
-Well what's going on?
-Well..........

Breaking The News

-I sat there by myself just thinking, I was
wondering how I would break the news when
he/she arrived.
-Hi, you said you needed to talk
-Hi, yes come and sit down.
-She/he looked really nervous, my mind was
spinning, why did she/he look so serious
-Can I get you a drink?
-No thank you.
-I didn't really want a drink either I was just

stalling because I didn't know how to break the news.......

I'm Home

-I'm home, did you hear me! I'm home.
-Oh hi.
-Oh hi is that it? Haven't you missed me?
-You've only been gone ten minutes.
-Have I?
-Yes you went out to get some custard creams.
-Custard creams?
-Yes to have with our cup of tea.
-Well it felt like a lot longer because you'll never believe what happened when I was out......

Let Me Explain

-Why are you looking at me like that?
-I just can't believe what I'm hearing
-Do you need to sit down?
-I think I need to lie down!
-It's not that shocking.…....Is it? Look here's a chair
-Let me explain again…..

Stuck

-How long do you think we'll be stuck here?
-Stop moaning
-I'm not moaning, I just want to get out of here

-I know we both do…….

High Up!

-It's an incredible feeling to be so high up,
look down there.
-I can't!

Who are they?
Where are they?
-Up a tree, up a mountain, in heaven, on top of
a roller coaster, on top of a building, in an
aeroplane
Why are they there?
Why can't the second character look down?

Open It

2/3 Characters
  1- I didn't come here to cause trouble.
  2- Why did you come?
  1- I came to give you this (they hand a
box/letter over)
  2/3- What is it?
  1- Open it….

CONTINUE….

Questions to consider….
Who are the characters?

Do you open it straight away? Which character actually opens it?
What happened directly before this?
What is in the box/letter?

Suggestions

Box-Money, weapon, nothing, puppy
Letter-Eviction notice, Death threat, Inheritance, Divorce papers, Legal papers, A letter from a long lost relative/old friend, A letter from prison, A note from someone you thought wouldn't find you.

Tips

To create tension try to include dramatic pauses/ moments of silence where the audience has to read faces and body language. Don't unravel the plot too quickly, make your audience think.

You could add a scene before this between B and C (if working in a 3) to establish their characters.

CLIMAX or ANTI-CLIMAX

- I saw you over there.
- That is because I was over there.
- Why didn't you just stay here?
- Because I have nothing else to say to you.
- Clearly you do cos you're here now.
- Don't start with me.
- Don't you speak to me like that.
- Like what?

- That! It wasn't my fault.
- Well whose fault was it?
- It was just an accident.
- Oh is that what you call it?
- Can't we just move on?
- So you call _____ 'Just an accident'

Don't Be a Baby

-Did you hear that?

-I was trying to shut it out.

-I heard it!

-I don't like it here.

-Why did you make us come here?

-I told you, for the adventure.

-Couldn't we have an adventure in a less scary location?

-Don't be a baby.

-If we get it on video we will be rich.

-How exactly?

-Well the news would want it for a start.

-No they wouldn't.

-Why not?

-Because they would say it's fake, everyone would.

-They can tell these days if it's fake and I'm telling you I've seen it before and it's very real.

-Now be brave and follow me. Shut the door behind you.

The Plan

-Well I think that went to plan.

-Really?

-Yes it seems to have worked.

-Then why are we stuck in here?

-Ah well you see I only planned the first bit.

-Right, so the crucial escape route bit you just thought we'd wing?

-I didn't realise the building would go into lock down when the alarm went off.

-OK so you thought we would rob the place then just stroll out the front door? I only did this because you said it was fool proof! And I needed the money.

-Just a small lapse in judgement. The next one will go better, we can plan it together.

-Next one!? The only place we will be planning to escape from is prison!

-Yer well that can be done too, I've seen it on the TV.

-I give up, can't believe I didn't realise your level of stupidity before I pulled a pair of your mothers tights over my head. Did you get that idea from TV too?

-Season 1 Episode 27 of CSI.

-Think you need to start watching the Prison Break box set!

SIRENS CAN BE HEARD

-Too late!

The Box

Four children sit staring at a box they've found hidden in the woods.

1- What do you think is in there?

2-I don't know.

3- I think it's a box of money.

4-Then we should hand to the police.

3-We should spend it more like!

1-I think it's an ancient mystical object.

2-It might curse us!

1-Don't be ridiculous, you've read too many stories.

4-I bet it's a magical game that transports you into different situations.

3-And brings animals from the jungle rampaging through your house!!

1-You've watched Jumanji too many times!

2-What if it's a body?

1-Stop being so negative! Besides it's not big enough for a body.

2-A head?

3-Yep well done that's more positive! (Sarcastically).

2-If you all thought it was something good you would have opened it already.

(The box moves)

4-Oh my days! Did you see that?

2-I can't look.

1-Open your eyes, that thing just moved.

3-Right one of us needs to open that thing.

1-I vote you!

3-Me? Why me?

1-You're the bravest!

3-Right finders keepers, if its money it's mine!!

1,2,4- Deal!!

(3 opens the box) continue…

Contrasting Scene's/Split Staging
SCENE 1

Parent 1- What time do you call this?

Kid 1- I'm only ten minutes late.

Parent 1- Don't even try and give me the
broken watch excuse, you're one hour late,
I've been worried sick.

Kid 1 – Sorry I lost track of time.

Parent 1 – You are always sorry. I bet you've
been out with that new
mate of yours again!

Kid 1 – So what.

Parent 1 – Don't speak to me like that, that
group of so called friends are bad news.

Kid 1- Give me a break will you, you would
rather have me locked away in my room
forever.

SCENE 2

Parent 2 – Late again.

Kid 2 – Yer no big deal.

Parent 2 – To be honest I've been too busy watching the tele to notice.

Kid 2 – What's in to eat?

Parent 2 – You should've brought some chips in with you.

Kid 2 – Got no money have I?

Parent 2 – Don't start that again I'm skint, borrow some off your new mate, their family is loaded.

Kid 2 – Yer whatever!

CONTRASTING OUTCOMES.

A- I looked at you and I knew

B- What?

A- I just knew straight away

B- Straight away? What are you going on about?

A- I knew you weren't telling me everything

B- Are you calling me a liar?

A- Your words not mine. I just need to know the whole story

B- You seriously don't...

Continue.......

Create 2 contrasting endings e.g. one comical, one serious.

<u>Nursery Rhyme Scripts</u>

<u>Don't Touch My Tarts!</u>

Queen of Hearts & Old King Cole

Queen of Hearts: DO NOT TOUCH MY TARTS!!

 (To audience)Do you hear me! They are for someone very special....

Old King Cole: Who your majesty?

Queen of Hearts: Me!

Old King Cole: Would you mind if I tasted one? I've heard great things about your   Jam tart recipe.

Queen: From who? I have never shared my recipe with anyone!!

King: From you.

Queen: Ah yes, it's true my recipe is the best in the land.

King: Well that's good because guess what...

Queen: I'm the Queen I don't do guessing!

King: sometimes guessing can be fun.

109

Queen: I don't do fun.

King: Of course you don't.

Queen: Well spit it out.

King: I've entered you for The Great British Bake Off!

Queen: You did what?????

King: I've entered you for The Great British Bake Off!

Queen: What was the point in that? I would obviously win.

King: I thought it would be fun.

Queen: I don't do fun!!!

(She turns to the audience)

Queen: Where are my tarts?! Which one of you has stolen my tarts?!

Miss Muffet in Therapy.

Miss Muffet, Dr. Foster & Incy Whincy
Spider

Miss Muffet: I just don't like Spiders.

Dr Foster: What did they ever do to you?

Miss Muffet: They scare me, all those legs and
they crawl so fast.

Dr Foster: And how do you think Incy feels
about this?

Miss Muffet: I don't know I've never even
spoken to him.

Dr Foster: Exactly. Incy is part of this
community too and I think you are hurting his
feeling by running away every time he
approaches you.

Miss Muffet: Why would he approach me if
it's not just to frighten me.

Dr Foster: Maybe he wants to be your friend.
The only way you will recover from your
arachnophobia is to face it head on. Which is
why I've asked Incy to join us.

(Miss Muffet starts taking deep breaths as the
door opens and Incy enters) Continue the
scene.....

The Hill

Jack, Jill and Mary Mary Quite Contrary

Jack: Jill! Jill come on we need to collect some water from the well.

Jill: But Jack I'm in the middle of a game of chess with Mary, although she is being rather contrary!

Mary: I am not, but I know the rules and you're not playing correctly.

Jill : (To audience) I think she's cheating!

Mary: I heard that!

Jack: Jill come on I can't manage by myself.

Jill: Ok I'm coming, I'm coming.

Mary: Any excuse to give up, just because you're losing.

Jill: We will finish this later!

Mary: If I have time, I might be busy in my garden.

Jill: You're so difficult; I think it's you who is scared of losing, scared of being wrong.

Jack: Jill!!!!!

Jill: Ok, Ok. Jack you're always in such a hurry. You keep racing around like that you'll end up having a nasty accident!

Jack: That's very unlikely Jill I've been up and down this hill hundreds of times and never even spilt a drop of water.

An Important Job

Humpty Dumpty & Little Bo Peep

Humpty: Help! Somebody help!

Bo Peep: Is everything ok Humpty?

Humpty: No Bo everything is not ok. I have been sitting up here for so long now that I want to get down and see the world.

Bo Peep: But Humpty you do such a great job protecting us all, we need someone like you to watch over nursery rhyme land.

Humpty: But it's so lonely up here.

Bo Peep: Do you remember when my Baaa-bra went missing and I couldn't find her anywhere? It was you Humpty that spotted her, and alerted the kings men who brought her to safety.

Humpty: It is an important job isn't it?

Bo Peep: Egg-sactly!!

Alphabet Script

-Alex how are you?
-Better than I was thank you.
-Can you keep a secret?
-Definitely! I love a good secret
-Excellent (whispers)
-For goodness sake Alex.
-Great isn't it?
-Hardly!
-If you can't be supportive leave me alone.
-Just think about it first
-Kick me when I'm down why don't you!
-Lets just put this in perspective.
-My perspective is perfectly in place!
-Not really if you're considering going ahead with this.
-Oh right so you don't want me to be happy
-Please don't be like that.
-Quick to judge though aren't you?!
-Right I'm done just don't ask me my opinion in future.
-So at what point did I ask for your opinion?
-Try to see the bigger picture.
-Understandably you're a bit jealous.
-Very funny.
-Why then are you being so negative?
-(e)Xtra caution that is all, I'm worried about you.
-You should just be happy that I've moved on, and keep your opinion to yourself.
-Zero opinion from now on!!!!

Trouble in the Enchanted Forest

Fairy: Morning Pixie, Elf, I have to speak to you both about something.

Elf: If it is about the attack on the east side of the enchanted forest.

Pixie: We know!

Fairy: So what shall we do about it?

Elf: We don't even know what is causing the trees to fall.

Pixie: I think it is a big, ugly monstrous giant who is coming to gobble us all up!

Elf/Fairy: Pixie!!

Pixie: well what else could it be?

Fairy: I heard a rumble like thunder last night and when I peeked out of the window another tree had fallen.

Elf: I think we should hide in the bushes this afternoon and see for ourselves.

Pixie: You will have to take that silly crown off Fairy, if that catches the light we'll be sure to get caught, then we will be the first to get eaten by the giant!

Fairy: First of all this crown is elegant not silly! Second of all there is NO GIANT!

Later that day……..In the bushes….

Elf: Pixie will you keep still you're going to give us away.

Pixie: This is a prickly bush!

Fairy: Look, look at that it's a, it's a….

Elf: It's a giant!

Pixie: Told you!!

Elf: A giant with a ginormous metal arm….. with teeth.

Pixie: Run for your lives!!

Fairy: Am I the bravest here? (She stands and shouts) Hey you! Leave our forest alone you big bully.

Elf: She's cracked!

Pixie: She's going to be his starter!

Elf: I'm a little concerned about his main meal and dessert! I'm with you Pixie….RUN!

Wizardry School

Child - Mum, Dad there's something important I want to tell you.

Mum - What is it?

Child - Well I think you better both sit down.

Dad - You're getting us worried now, has something happened at school?

Child - Not exactly. You see the thing is.... I want to go to the school of Wizardry?

Mum - School of what?

Child - Wizardry.

Dad - You've been watching too much Harry Potter!

Mum - There's no such place.

Child - Well I've done my research and I'm telling you there is.

Dad - You need to learn proper subjects at school.

Mum - You need to stop dreaming and start taking school more seriously, real school that is!

Child - You need to take me and my dreams more seriously!

Dad - It's out of the question young man/lady.

Child - Fine you've given me no
choice... stand back!
With a shake of my wand,
From here to beyond,
I cast this spell over you,
So you believe what I say is true.

Mum - Well I think that's a wonderful idea,
our son/daughter going to wizardry school,
can you just imagine it, the neighbours will be
so jealous.

Dad - A truly marvellous opportunity!

Mum - We better get your bags packed, the
sooner the better. Our son/daughter a real life
wizard!

Mum & Dad - We are so proud.

Christmas Dinner

SANTA: What do you mean no Turkey?

MRS CLAUS: I just thought a change might be nice.

SANTA: But it's Xmas, it's tradition.

MRS CLAUS: And I thought this year we could be a little different.

SANTA: Now love I don't mean to be rude, and I know you do the cooking but it is Christmas and on Christmas day I expect Turkey.

MRS CLAUS: You expect!

SANTA: Well I am Santa.

MRS CLAUS: Don't I know it.

SANTA: And when 'Santa' has been racing around the world in order to deliver all the children's presents he gets HUNGRY!

MRS CLAUS: I didn't say you wouldn't eat, I just fancied something different.

SANTA: Well I don't.

MRS CLAUS: Well you cook then!

SANTA: After my busiest working night of the year?!

MRS CLAUS: Your ONLY working night of the year.

SANTA: It's a very important job.

MRS CLAUS: OK your royal festiveness! and my job isn't important? I take care of you every day of the year, I feed and clothe the elves, I practically run a hotel and I never get a break. Well Mr C I need a day off so it's settled takeaway it is!!

Night of the Reindeer

Dasher-Always rushing
Dancer-Elegant
Prancer-Perfectionist
Vixen-Flirty
Comet-Factual
Cupid-Romantic
Donner-Organised
Blitzen-Clever
Rudolf-Not very bright but loveable

Dancer-Will you slow down Dasher, you're
going to cause an accident.

Dasher-We need to get around the whole
world in one night, there's every reason to
dash.

Vixen-Dasher don't listen to Dancer, Dasher
by name, dashing by nature.

Blitzen-I think you've actually made him
blush.

Cupid-Do I detect love in the air?

Dasher-Cupid!

Cupid-I'm named after the Greek God of love
for a reason.

Vixen-I don't need any help from you Cupid, I
know how to impress the stags.

Donner-Sure you do. Rudolf you're quiet tonight.

Rudolf-Just doing my job Donner, guiding the way. Comet, what's your forecast on the night skies this Christmas Eve.

Comet-Pretty clear for most of the world, we may even get to see the northern lights over Iceland.

Cupid-How romantic, eh Dasher.

Prancer-Stop teasing him Cupid

Cupid-You just keep the timing Prancer.

Prancer-Everything In counts of eight eh dancer.

Dancer-Absolutely Prancer, we need perfect timing. I could've been on dancing with the stars you know.

Prancer-Sure you could.

Vixen-I'd like to dance with you.

Cupid-You'd dance with any deer.

Vixen-Watch you're mouth Cupid, you're just jealous of my good looks and stunning antlers.

Comet-Ladies please. Just enjoy the night's sky. Look a shooting star.

Rudolf-Beautiful.

Dancer-Sure is Rudolf. Like dancing stars.

Rudolf-Dancing stars.

Blitzen-Hey guys I don't mean to panic any one bit aren't we missing something? Or should I say someone.

Donner-Role call. (They all respond with 'present' after each name) Dasher? Dancer? Prancer? Comet? Cupid? Me? Blitzen? Rudolf?

Dasher-Hey what about Vix?

Vixen-Yer guys what about me?

Doner-Doh! (Meaning Doe)

Vixen-Oh ha ha!

Rudolf-I don't get it.

Blitzen-He's got no I deer! (Laughs)

Vixen-Doe, Doe a deer a female deer!

Rudolf-Oh.

Comet-How long have you been waiting to crack that one Donner?

Dasher-So we are all present and correct.

Vixen-Present!

Rudolf-Present....present......Presents! We have no presents!!

Blitzen-And that's because.... anyone? We are missing?..... anyone.... anyone?
All-Santa!

Dancer-We left Santa!

All-Oh deer!

Ainsfield's Thirty Fifth Production

Director- Welcome to Ainsfield's thirty fifth anniversary production of...

Mildred- Where do you want me?

Director- And you are?

Mildred- Mildred.

Director-Ah yes Mildred, and you are auditioning for?

Mildred-Witch one.

Director- Yes that's what I'm asking you.

Mildred- Witch one.

Director- Yes which one are you auditioning for? Which is your role of preference in our thirty fifth anniversary production of...

Mildred- I'm here to audition for Witch one.

Director- Witch one? Do you mean the Wicked Witch of the West?

Mildred- No I mean witch one, should I start?.... Double, double toil and ...

Director- That's Macbeth.

Mildred- No it's Witch one.

Director- Yes Macbeth!

Mildred- No it's definitely by Shakespeare.

Director- Yes William Shakespeare who wrote Macbeth.

Mildred- Ah yes then you're right. I'm here to be your witch one from Macbeth by Mr William Shakespeare.

Director- That's nice Mavis.

Mildred-Mildred.

Director- That's nice Mildred but this is an audition for the Ainsfield's Amateur Dramatics society thirty fifth Anniversary production of The Wizard of Oz.

Mildred- Could you maybe do it in Shakespearean language.

Director- Erm no Mavis...Mildred, I could not, I will do it as the playwright has written it.

Mildred- Well that's not very creative is it?

Director- OK Mildred if thou wouldst like to leaveth through the dooreth I will get on with my MUSICAL which I can promise you has no connection to the works of Shakespeare,

and will be A.A.D.S's 35th anniversary
production complete with a yellow brick road
made of real bricks, flying monkeys that fly
and no Shakespearean witches.

(Mildred exits in a huff)

Directors- Flaming thespians! Next!....

Ghosts

MICHAEL: Let's go!

JESS: Where are we going Mike?

MICHAEL: I've told you we're going to the woods.

JESS: Can't we go somewhere else?

MICHAEL: Are you scared?

JESS: No... I just get bored listening to your stupid ghost stories.

MICHAEL: Do you want to hear one now....

JESS: No!

MICHAEL: They're true you know, Dad says.

JESS: I don't want to go Michael. Mum said we had to be home by six.

MICHAEL: You're such a scaredy cat! Look I brought Dads camera, if we can get a picture of the ghost we'll be famous!

JESS: I don't want to be famous, I just want my tea.

MICHAEL: What's that?

JESS: What?

MICHAEL: That smoke coming from that house? It's meant to be empty!

JESS: Mikey we have to go home.

MICHAEL HAS ALREADY WALKED TOWARDS THE HOUSE.

JESS: Mikey stop. Where are you going?

MICHAEL: come on Jess keep up, we haven't got all day!

JESS: Michael!

MICHEAL: Jess!

JESS: Argh! You are going to get us in so much trouble.

JESS RELUCTANTLY FOLLOWS. THEY APPROACH THE BIG WOODEN DOOR OF THE ABANDONED HOUSE.

JESS: Come on lets go back home!

MICHAEL KNOCKS ON THE DOOR. THE DOOR OPENS BUT THERE IS NO ONE THERE.

MICHAEL: well, that was creepy.

JESS: That's why I think we should leave.

MICHAEL ENTERS.

MICHAEL: Hello! Anyone here? Hello.

*A SWOOP OF WIND SLAMS THE DOOR
BEHIND THEM. LIGHTS COME UP ON A
COUPLE BY A LOG FIRE.*

HENRY: Did you hear that love?

LIZA: It's just the wind Henry.

HENRY: No I think it was the door.

LIZA: You've got a vivid imagination
Henry. It's windy out there tonight.

JESS: Ssh! Mikey there's someone in here.

MICHAEL: I know, I told you....Ghosts!

JESS: Pack it in you're scaring me now.

HENRY: I'll check it out.

MICHAEL: I'll check it out.

JESS: Don't leave me here.

LIZA: Henry it's nothing relax

The Loft

Jez-I'm telling you I heard it on the news, the infection is heading this way. It started down South and is on its way to Yorkshire.

Ian-Are you kidding me?

Jez-No I'm not, that's why we need to get the family together and make a space in the loft.

Ian-The loft?

Jez-Yes I figure we need to be high up, you know in case of any manifestations.

Ian-Manifestations?

Jez-Do I need to spell it out?

Ian-Erm, maybe.

Jez-Zombie manifestation.

Ian-Zombie?

Jez-This Ian is no normal infection! We are talking Zombie apocalypse here.

Ian-Are you sure it was the news you were watching?

Jez-Look we are wasting time here, you gather as many bottles of water and tins of food as possible, don't forget the can opener. I'm on barricade duty, no sucker is getting anywhere near our loft. But look you need to keep this quiet the loft will only hold five people.

Scene 2

Jez-And you chose to bring him because?

Ian-No one else would take me seriously.

Jez-Jeez Ian how many people did you ask?

Ian-Terry was my fourth.

Jez-Great so when they all realise this is a real threat, they will all be fighting their way up here.

Ian-Sorry.

Terry- I've always wanted a real life adventure Jez.

Jez-Have you Terry? Well isn't that great.

Terry- Don't be like that Jez we're on the same side.

Jez- You're a crazy loon Terry.

Ian-Exactly Jez, every zombie apocalypse has its bat shit crazy character.

Jez-This isn't a flaming comic book Ian.

Terry-I brought these (he opens a case to reveal bows and arrows)

Jez-A right modern day Robin Hood you. (Beat) yer I guess you could be useful.

Ian- So what do we do now?

Jez-Wait.

Terry-Top Trumps anyone?

Ian-Not now Terry. I'm sure Jez has a plan he'd like to share with us.

Scene 3
They are playing top trumps

Ian-So mate what did the news actually say? We've been up here 4 hours 20 minutes and 35 seconds and nothing seems to be happening.

Jez-It started down South Ian the infections probably only just reached Birmingham. Zombies don't travel by car Ian, don't you watch The Walking Dead?

Ian-I'm still on season 2.

Terry-The farm, that's the best one. I've watched them all and I don't actually remember at any point Rick saying 'Come on gang let's hide in this Loft!'

Jez-Shut it psycho.

Ian- Calm down.

Jez-What did you bring him for?

Ian- I told you everyone else laughed.

Terry-And I was just up for the laugh.

Jez- You two morons will be laughing on the other side of your face when I kick your backsides down that hatch, and into the clutches of some gory hungry Zombies.

Ian- Anyway what happened to bringing your family?

Jez-Changed my mind about asking them.

Ian-They laughed at you didn't they.

Jez-It's your turn(beat) It is your turn Terry!

Terry- Darth Maul power 270.

(There's a sudden bang on the hatch, Terry loads his bow with an arrow)

Ian- Jeez what the hell's that?

Jez-They're here. This is it; they've got through the barricade.

Hannah- Open the hatch freaks.

Jez-Hannah?

Hannah-Jez open the hatch.

(He lets her in, she looks around then bursts out laughing)

Hannah-Aww this is cute Jeremy, are you boys having a sleep over.

Jez-Get lost.

Terry- Hi Hannah.

Hannah-Get lost Terry.

Jez-What do you want?

Hannah- I was bored, thought I'd come any see what my dozy brother and his dim wit mates were up to. Top Trumps whoa party on boys.

Boys- Get lost Hannah.

Hannah-Oh and Mum wants the can opener. So these two numb skulls believed your story?

Jez-You'll be sorry.

Hannah-Sorry to be related to you.

Jez-You can go now!

Hannah-Hi Ian.

Ian-Hey.

Hannah-You want me to stay don't you Ian.

Ian-Sure.

(Moaning can be heard.)

Jez-Did you hear that?

Terry-Yer.

Hannah-Was it you Terry? Is that you belly rumbling?

Jez-Shut up Hannah. Ian close the hatch it's happening.

Ensemble Work-Stichomythic Dialogue

-Hope
-fingers crossed
-four leaf clover
-rabbits foot
-ewww
-good luck to me
-could be life changing
-life changing
-anticipation
-my hearts racing
-d dum d dum d dum
-beating faster
-here we go
-this is it
-my life changing moment
-ball number 25
-check
-ball number 4
-check
-ball number 35
-Oh my days!
-check, check, check
-check again
-check
-ball number 43
-I can hardly believe this
-believe it
-ball number 11
-Check
-heart racing, pounding, beating out of my
chest
-cross everything

-everything crossed
-I missed it, oh my days! I missed it. What did they say?
-rewind! REWIND!!
-Ball number 14
-Did they say 14?
-14
-14!
-Time freezes!
-Slow motion takes over
-We celebrate
-Life changing
-Hello, I think I may have just won the jackpot
-25, 4, 35, 43, 11, 14
-Holy shhh
-shall we (leads centre stage)
-A dozen roses
-as requested
-The finest diamonds
-as demanded
-Three course meal madam/sir
-A new woman/man
-A changed person
-A person with so much more, yet so little
-Friends turn their backs
-Who cares I have more, more than you, and you
-Yet she/he has so much less
-Family feuds
-You gave her more than me, it's not fair
-I deserve more I'm your sister
-The ladies/fellas love me
-They love your bank balance
-I'm loved

-superficially
-I'm important
-I'm leaving you
-You're lonely
-I have everything
-You have nothing but heart ache ahead
-You've changed

Reacting to dialogue using only facial expression and body language. This could be recorded and played back for the students to react to.

Dialogue 1

What did you say? Look at me child! What did you say? How dare you speak to me like that, who do you think you are? Look at you all pathetic crying on the floor like a baby. You wouldn't have behaved like that if your mother had been around would you? But she's not around is she? And that's your fault. She left because of you, are you listening to me child? You are so pathetic. Look at me when I'm talking to you!! How dare you turn away from your father! You're a disgrace.

Dialogue 2

-Are you ok?
(No answer)
-Where do you live?
(No answer)
-Would you like me to call someone?
(Shakes head)
-What is your name?
(No answer)
-Are you hurt?
(No answer)
-I can't help you if you don't talk to me.
(Mumbles name)

141

-Sorry

(Repeats name)

-What's your surname?

(Shrugs)

-Is that your blood (name), are you hurt?

(Shakes head)

-Can you stand?

(Nods)

-Let me take you somewhere warm, it's cold out here and you're shivering.

(Shakes head, gets panicked)

-I'm not going to hurt you, I want to help. You can't stay out here all by yourself.

(She/he reluctantly stands)

The following is an extract from the play 'Who Needs Enemies.'

DEE JUMPS UP AND HASTILY GRABS THE PHONE.

DEE: Please.

CLAIRE: How can you be sure they're not hurt? You left the scene of an accident.

DEE: I'm sure.

CLAIRE: How can you be?

DEE: Stop it ok, I'm sure.

CLAIRE: How?

DEE: Because...

CLAIRE: (YELLING) Because what?

DEE: Because he's dead ok, he's dead!

CLAIRE IN SHOCK RETURNS SLOWLY TO SIT ON THE SOFA.

CLAIRE: (STUNNED) Jesus Christ!

DEE: It wasn't my fault.

CLAIRE: It never is.

DEE: I didn't see it coming.

CLAIRE: (INFURIATED) You were drunk!

BEAT

CLAIRE: You killed someone , and left them just bloody left them!

DEE: I didn't mean to.

CLAIRE: What, kill them or leave them? you are unbelievable. Where did the blood come from? It's not just from you Dee, tell me where the damn blood came from!

DEE: I checked the body.

CLAIRE: For what?... Money? Did you rob the poor sod!

DEE: For a pulse Claire, a pulse.

CLAIRE: Then you left, just got up and left them to rot?

DEE: No! Not exactly....

CLAIRE: What do you mean?

DEE: (DESPERATELY) I need your help, Claire you have to help me.

CLAIRE: I have spent my whole life helping you, digging you out of situations, but you've over stepped the mark this time. We need to ring the police, explain you were scared, tell them you're sorry for leaving the scene and take your punishment. You need to tell them where the other car and the body is.

DEE: I can't.

CLAIRE: Yes you can. You have to. They'll catch up with you eventually and the consequences will be worse.

DEE: You don't understand.

CLAIRE: You're right there.

DEE: You don't understand, I can't tell them where the body is.

CLAIRE: Why?

BEAT.

CLAIRE: Why?

BEAT.

CLAIRE: (ANGRILY) Jesus Christ. Why can't you tell them where the body is?

DEE: Because it's in my car!

CLAIRE: What?!

DEE: I somehow managed to get him in the boot.

CLAIRE: The boot! You're not a flaming gangster Dee! You idiot!

DEE: I know, I'm sorry.

CLAIRE: Sorry doesn't even begin to cover it.

Using poetry as a stimulus for debate,
devising scenes and monologues.

Capital Punishment.

"The death sentence" the judge did say,
As the jury voted him dead,
And as they left the court in silence,
The criminal hung his head.
Led off to the chamber,
He pleaded "I'm insane",
But the executioner ignored him,
And he cried his last cry in vain.

He'd said his last prayer to God,
And forgiveness he had pleaded,
But was he really sorry for,
All the children he'd mistreated.
He had committed a serious sin,
But did he deserve to die?
Couldn't he just be jailed for life?
For this horrific and vulgar crime.

So, put this man to his death,
But surely that's a sin,
To have to lower yourself to this,
And commit the same crime as him.
Two wrongs don't make a right,
And if you murder this man,
Then do you deserve to die also?
Should this sentence be banned?

If you think the death penalty,
Will forever stop the crime,
Then you are sadly mistaken,
You should imprison for life time.
No one has the right to take a life,
No matter what they've done,
There's more effective ways to solve,
The things we know are wrong.

Self Destruction.

There was a world that was created,
Many years ago.
That same world we destructed,
As we watched the happiness erode.
And as we looked upon this slow death,
And watched the time tick by.
The world we took for granted,
Slowly withered and it died.

No one really bothered to think,
Of the future it would hold.
And the children who would have to live,
In a world their parents sold.
The problems of the world,
We humans are aware.
But it's too late and all is lost,
Because no one really cares.

We had a selfish attitude,
Of wanting more and more.
Until we slowly did destroy,
The garden we were born.

148

And because of greed and money,
With both we're always hooked.
We didn't stop to think,
One day we'd self destruct.

And now that time has past,
And the problems have arisen.
Our children have been born,
Into an environmental prison.
Where all they'll ever really know,
Of a world that was once great.
Is when their elders tell that ugliness,
Came when they tempted fate.

This is a story about the world,
And how you should think twice.
Before we all destroy the land,
With an evil man made device.
And how a thought for the future,
Wouldn't be a thought to pass.
And a thought for our environment,
Would help to make it last.

Lightning Source UK Ltd.
Milton Keynes UK
UKHW040829070622
404062UK00001B/136